Surviving grief doesn't mean that you no longer miss the one who died. That person is in your life forever, but his role in your life must change. You can continue to love him, but the love eventually becomes a smaller part of your life. You must say the final good-bye to him so that you can move on. You must let go with love.

LETTING GO WITH LOVE

"A self-help book that offers practical approaches to dealing with loss and grief."
—*The Arizona Daily Star*

"Its completeness and straightforward, readable quality can only be done by someone who's been there."
—*Ernest F. Pecci, M.D.*

"A sensitive, curative resource for the benefit of the terminally ill."
—*ALA Booklist*

D1469120

LETTING GO WITH LOVE:
The Grieving Process

Nancy O'Connor, Ph.D.

BANTAM BOOKS

NEW YORK · TORONTO · LONDON · SYDNEY · AUCKLAND

LETTING GO WITH LOVE: THE GRIEVING PROCESS
A Bantam Book / published by arrangement with
La Mariposa Press

PRINTING HISTORY
La Mariposa Press edition published 1984
Bantam edition / September 1989

Acknowledgment is made to Medic Publishing Company and Amy Hillyard Jensen for permission to reprint the material in Appendix A, and to Concern for Dying, 250 W. 57th Street, New York , NY 10107 for permission to reprint "The Living Will."

Bantam Books are published by Bantam Books, a division of Bantam Doubleday Dell Publishing Group, Inc. Its trademark, consisting of the words "Bantam Books" and the portrayal of a rooster, is Registered in U.S. Patent and Trademark Office and in other countries. Marca Registrada. Bantam Books, 666 Fifth Avenue, New York, New York 10103.

PRINTED IN THE UNITED STATES OF AMERICA

O   0 9 8 7 6 5 4 3 2 1

ACKNOWLEDGMENTS

This book would not have been possible without the cooperation, encouragement, and support of other people. I want to thank Carol Sowell for her brilliant editorial work, and her willingness to extend herself beyond a normal work-for-pay basis to research markets and to educate me on the ups and downs of writing and publishing.

Many people facilitated my personal growth and professional interest in grief work. Significant among these are Drs. Frances Scott and Saul Toobert of the University of Oregon. Their creative teaching went far beyond the traditional academic format. Their students learned not only intellectually, but also grew emotionally and personally.

Over the years many clients have been teachers for me. They have given me their trust in knowing that I care and respect them in times of need.

Finally, I wish to thank Dr. Elisabeth Kubler-Ross for taking time in her busy schedule to review the manuscript and to endorse the book.

DEDICATION

To all the people who have come into my life and left again. To those who have loved me and allowed me to love them. Through these relationships I have learned, grown and grieved their loss. Some were more lengthy than others and emotionally mixed with joy and pain, especially my parents, my grandparents and my infant daughter, Mary Margaret.

TABLE OF CONTENTS

INTRODUCTION

WHAT THIS BOOK IS ABOUT: WHAT IT CAN DO FOR YOU

When a person dies, his suffering is over, at least in life on earth. But those who are still living are faced with huge pressures, devastating trauma, important decisions, and powerful emotions. The survivors' suffering or grieving has just begun. The attention of friends and relatives has been focused on the one who was dying. But now the ones most closely affected by the death need the concern and caring of family and friends.

Most of us don't know what grief will be like until we experience it firsthand. We expect to be sad and hurt, but we may be surprised to feel other emotions like anger and guilt. We may discover that after someone dies, our relationships with others change. Our families and friendships may not be the same because of the changes we undergo after a loss.

In recent years, research has shown that there are identifiable patterns of emotions in grief. Knowing what those are can help you recognize that the turmoil and pain you feel are part of healing the injury that death has inflicted.

When a person can deal successfully with change, he

can reach a higher level of growth, sensitivity, and understanding of himself and others. The death of someone important in our lives is a change, a major one, sometimes a sudden one. But change, even painful change, is an important, necessary part of being alive.

Loss of someone through death is a particularly painful change, especially if you felt deep love toward that person. The more intense your love for her, your dependence on and hopes for her, the more it will hurt to lose her or him.

There's no getting around the pain; you must get through it. You can't avoid it, if you are truly alive to your emotions. Avoiding the emotions of grief is a dangerous business that can lead to illness and serious distress. Worst of all, not dealing with our emotions leaves us stuck psychologically, unable to change and grow. Continuing to dwell on the anger or depression or guilt that arises during grief would be like having an open cut on your skin that continues to bleed and leaves the injured flesh exposed. Not only does the wound never heal, but eventually infection sets in and leads to worse problems.

So it is with grief. Progress in healing happens gradually, but eventually it is completed. If healing is blocked, infection, in the form of emotional damage, arrested growth, and inability to live life fully, takes over.

Healing is accomplished by grief work. It's work because you can't approach it passively; you have to manage it. You will sometimes feel pain and resistance. At times you think that you'll never recover from this loss. But by doing the work—experiencing, expressing and managing the emotions that you feel—you *will* recover. You'll be able to move from the past, to live in the present and envision the future.

Surviving grief doesn't mean that you no longer miss the one who died. That person is in your life forever, but his role in your life must change. You can continue to love him, but the love eventually becomes a smaller part of your life. You must say the final goodbye to him so that you can move on. You must let him go with love.

I came to write this book out of many years of experience as a counselor and a human being. My own life has contained a number of losses. My father committed suicide when I was a young woman. I had a baby who died. I have said goodbye to dear friends who died from accidents or illness. And, while I was writing this book, my mother died after several years of failing health. I've also experienced loss through divorce, moving, watching my children grow up and other personal and professional changes.

In counseling people who are grieving for their own losses, I've been able to draw on my experiences to assure them that others have felt the same kinds of pain and that one *does* survive. I've learned much from my clients about suffering and surviving. Now I'd like to share that knowledge and understanding with you.

People going through grief have some things in common, such as the stages of the grief process. The first three chapters cover these universal experiences. The material in these chapters can help you with any grieving situations, whether for a death in your own life, or when a friend has a loss, or when you are faced with a change through illness, separation or financial crisis.

The next five chapters go into more detail about specific losses. Although grieving follows a predictable pattern, the experience of losing a wife after fifty years of marriage is not the same as the death of a teen-age son or a best friend. Each chapter looks at some of the special problems connected with specific losses, while also containing material that may apply in other situations.

The chapter on death of the self is written to offer aid to those who have a terminal illness, or those close to someone who must face death soon. Another chapter looks at the unique circumstances facing the survivors of a suicide.

The last two chapters are meant to help you recognize the patterns in your life that may influence how *you* process grief. You can identify your own ways of coping with change and use this knowledge to heal yourself and to choose to continue living. The most important thing I can tell you is that you *can* choose. Life can go on in a rich, exciting way—*you* are the one who has the power to make it happen.

You may decide to read only parts of this book right now, especially if you're groping for ways to handle a particular recent loss. You may find there are parts you'll come back to later. You may even find sections you don't understand or don't believe. But later those ideas will mean more to you, when you have moved from one stage of grief to another. The book can help you be better prepared for deaths in the future or to complete your grief for a long-ago death which you may never have released.

My wish is to help you understand your process as you grieve, to realize that grief has a progressive course and to assist in knowing that through all your current pain *you will survive* and, in time, once more experience joy in living.

Emotional reactions to the death of a loved one follow a fairly defined course. By giving in to these feelings and letting them occur in their natural timing, and being aware of things you may do that block the process, healing will take place. Death is a wound—a severe and painful psychological wound. As with any injury to the physical body, healing requires tender loving care, gentleness, and time.

Grieving is all the feelings, reactions and changes that occur during the process of healing. You have a choice of how you will heal yourself, although it may not feel like a conscious choice in the beginning. One choice is to allow yourself to grieve, to feel all of the anguish and fear and pain as they present themselves to you. This is the choice that eventually allows you to go on with your life.

The other choice is a move toward non-feeling, toward your own psychological death and eventually toward your physical death. Previous grieving patterns and individual personality traits contribute to the way you will naturally react to bereavement in the beginning. These are your natural predispositions, but you *can* change if old patterns do not serve you well.

What's most important in learning to live with loss is letting yourself feel. Allow! Allow! Allow! Allow yourself to feel—to experience—to live again.

To fear death, gentlemen, is nothing other than to think oneself wise when one is not; for it is to think one knows what one does not know. No man knows whether death may not even turn out to be the greatest of blessings for a human being; and yet people fear it as if they knew for certain that it is the greatest of evils.

—*Socrates*

CHAPTER ONE

WHEN SOMEONE DIES

We live in a death-defying society. We fight and resist death; we hurry through our mourning and rush to get back to "normal." This attitude makes the grieving process more difficult and confusing for the survivors because it denies the importance and depth of their feelings.

Not so long ago, death was experienced as a natural part of the life cycle. Most people died at home surrounded by family and friends. Children were around the dying process and included in the funeral and burial rituals.

Today, many of our efforts to prolong life or minimize grieving emotionally shortchange everyone involved. It can leave us with unresolved pain.

The Depersonalization of Dying

Over sixty percent of us die in institutions such as hospitals and nursing homes. With the advances of modern medicine and the "heroic" measures available to extend life, most people are whisked off to the nearest hospital emergency room and turned over to strangers to be shocked, monitored, punctured, poked, and pounded by intimidating pieces of machinery while they are dying. Family and friends are not only excluded from the presence of the loved one, they often are denied the right to make decisions about what measures are to be taken to continue life. Nor is the dying person consulted or advised of what is being done to her or him.

Death is viewed as an enemy to be conquered at all costs, rather than a natural, inevitable part of being human, being alive.

After death, the body is taken to a mortuary or funeral parlor where strangers embalm, dress, perfume, and make it up with cosmetics to give the appearance of still looking alive. More denial.

By contrast, in the late 19th century less than twenty percent of Americans died in hospitals. The common occurrence was for people to die in the home where they had lived most of their lives. People often knew when they were dying, unless death was caused by an accident or sudden illness. The dying person had a chance to finish the emotional business of his or her life in familiar surroundings. In the last hours, vigilant family members and friends circled around to say goodbye.

Not all deaths were expected then or now. Life before advanced medical technology also included many sudden, untimely deaths. Prized animals were slaughtered for food. Babies and young children died of childhood diseases or accidents. Women died in childbirth; men were killed in wars and accidents.

After the death, family members took care of the burial. The women washed and dressed the body, while the men made the casket and dug the grave. What a wonderful opportunity to complete obligations to the departing family member and to come to terms with the finality of the person's life—and to say goodbye with love and care!

The body was often buried on the grounds of the home where survivors would continue to regard the dead person as part of their environment. During the first days after the death, friends and neighbors brought food and support for the mourners.

In the old, rural way of death and mourning, the close involvement of each family member with the dying one helped survivors to view death as natural and accept it as part of the life cycle. Not a strange and horrible occurrence, but a part of life. Unfortunately we have lost the personal contact in the death rituals.

Our cultural denial of death began to grow as people moved to cities to work in factories. Hospitals became a place to go to seek cures. The medical profession began to view death as a failure, and stepped up efforts to fight the "enemy" of death with increasingly sophisticated technology such as drugs, surgery and machinery. These prolong the last days or months of life, even though the survivor is often semi-conscious or unconscious much of the time.

As more people went to hospitals their impending death was greeted with denial, first by the medical staff, then by their families. The dying person began to view death as the enemy and to struggle against it. The *fight* to live in the face of impossible odds has always been the last battle lost. The final failure.

Communication between the loved one and family members changed. Truth was changing. In an attempt to "spare the feelings" of the dying person, lies crept into the dying process. Doctors lied, nurses lied, family members lied and eventually the dying person lied. The subject became taboo, veiled in secrecy and deceit. Everyone began to pretend that death was something unreal, an illusion. Relatives no longer keep watch by the person's bedside, but they come and go, according to hospital visiting hours.

Yet many people are afraid of dying alone or among strangers, unloved and uncared for. We also fear being dependent or undergoing intolerable pain, choking or suffocating to death. With the prevailing denial of death among families these are reasonable fears especially to the lonely residents of nursing homes or the seriously ill person in a hospital bed, wondering when his loved ones will come again to visit.

In an attempt to reverse this trend of death in unfamiliar surroundings the Hospice Movement was started in England in the 1960's, and is gaining popularity in the United States. The Hospice principle advocates dying at home again, surrounded by family members. The staff provides support and information to the entire family; with counseling they encourage open, honest communication. They also believe in reasonable pain control, so that the dying person can be as comfortable as possible to the end.

In the United States, Hospices were supported by the National Cancer Institute a few years ago as demonstration projects. They became so popular that most cities have a program now. If you are interested, call your local city or county health department to see if there is one in your community.

With our busy lives, greater mobility, and separation of family members, death is no longer a part of our lives. Even if a member of the family is soon to die, it is not part of the day-to-day reality for a son or daughter who lives 2,000 miles away. The distant child or sibling doesn't participate in the imminent death and may feel it is happening to someone else, a stranger. They may attend the funeral, but it has a touch of unreality and lacks true connectedness.

Nonetheless, a funeral brings the idea of death uncomfortably close. When we see, or are involved in some way with, another person's dying, we experience a sense of loss of ourselves. We start to think of our own future death. We mourn for the deceased one and for ourselves. Part of the intensely strong feelings and confusion experienced during the grieving period comes from these mixed emotions, of missing the other person, and at the same time, being glad it is he who is dead, not me.

This self-consciousness is why friends and neighbors are often uncomfortable in expressing their condolences to you. Subconsciously, they are glad they are not going through the pain of losing a loved one. In watching your grief they are forced to imagine themselves in a similar situation, to think of how it would be to lose a parent, spouse, or a child. They also may begin to think of the limits of their own lives. They may be sincerely sympathetic with you, but they feel guilty for being glad that it is not their loss. These conflicting emotions are a natural part of thinking about death. Recognizing them can help you deal with a friend's mourning or your own.

Denying Our Emotions

The taboo of talking about death in our country has far-reaching implications for the dying, as well as for the survivors. Those nearing the end of their lives are cheated of completing unfinished business in relationships, such as saying goodbye, and asking for or bestowing forgiveness for perceived wrongs during their lives. It is most difficult to accomplish these necessary tasks if the one you are trying to talk to responds to your efforts by saying, "Now, you are not going to die. I don't want to hear another word."

Denying death may seem to be a way of easing our grief, but in fact it has the opposite result. When we deny dying we also deny an important part of authentic living. Death is a natural consequence of living. No one escapes it. Life is full of a variety of experiences for all of us. We have good times and bad times. Times of sadness, disappointment, frustration, sorrow, as well as times of joy, love and happiness. Death is another experience.

Most of us seek happiness and avoid painful or negative feelings. We live in the foggy myth that happiness is the only acceptable state of existence. The French philosopher Philippe Aries notes that it has become the "moral duty and social obligation to contribute to the collective happiness by avoiding any cause for sadness or boredom, by appearing to be happy even if in the depths of despair."

Continual happiness is the unspoken mandate of our lives, but it is an unrealistic goal. No one is happy all of the time. It is through the painful experiences of our lives that we grow, become more sensitive, empathetic and caring for others in similar situations and learn more about our own values and emotions.

Illness and death are not "happy" events, and because they contrast so sharply with our irrational pursuit of happiness, they are consequently denied in ourselves and in others.

Mourning is thought to be morbid. People are uncomfortable around someone grieving. It is very difficult for people grieving today to find the necessary support to aid them in resolving their grief. It is risky to ask someone to listen to your weeping and wailing. You may be rejected by friends who don't know how to help you. In spite of these fears, I encourage you to reach out and ask for help when you want it. There are loving, caring people who will respond to your needs. If family and friends aren't the answer, another option is joining a self-help group where people in similar situations share their feelings, fears and frustration. There are several around and new ones are being formed all the time. Some are listed in Appendix B.

All across the country there are services and programs for widows that provide information about insurance, financial investments, community resources, and emotional support. Another group, Parents of Murdered Children, was formed in 1978 in Cincinnati, and chapters are starting in other cities. Members say that they found a lack of support elsewhere, that they feel let down by families, friends, co-workers, members of their churches, and the criminal justice system. They come together twice a week and help each other deal with the anguish and pain of their grieving.

Another national group called Compassionate Friends has chapters in several cities. This group supports parents who have lost a child of any age from infancy to adulthood.

These are only a few examples of such groups; there are others for survivors of suicide, for parents with terminally ill children and so on. If you don't find an organization in your community to meet your needs, start one. It is much easier to share your grief than try to go it alone. You will help yourself and others at the same time.

Steps in Saying Goodbye

Mourning is not a disease. It is a normal and natural process that allows the separation to slowly become a reality. In those first few dreadful days, when you feel numb with shock and disbelief, the ritual of the funeral serves the purpose of keeping you busy, of bringing support from loved ones, and of giving you time to begin to come to terms with your loss.

The ceremony of the funeral makes accepting the reality of the death a little easier. The activity involved in notifying relatives and friends, choosing a funeral home, a casket, clothes, music, and the type of burial

are all necessary and time-consuming. You may go
through these preparations in a dream-like state, but the
busyness keeps you involved in being practical, making
decisions, and staying in touch with ongoing everyday
responsibilities.

The ritual of the funeral provides a safe and supportive environment for those who had the closest connections with the dead person. It is a place to express their
feelings and to receive support from others.

The funeral is the time to acknowledge and honor
your loved one publicly. The eulogy is generally deliv-
ered by a priest, rabbi, minister, or member of the
family. This is the final farewell to the physical body of
the person you know and loved; now only memories
remain.

Some funeral directors understand the need for a more
personal goodbye and will let families who request it be
involved in the preparation of the body. Remember—burial
rituals and funerals are for the living, a separation rite. A
chance to come to terms with the reality of the death. An
ending.

Memorial services with a closed casket and a favorite
photograph of the deceased are becoming more popular. I recently attended a lovely memorial service for the
mother of a good friend where special personal belongings were on hand, including her golf clubs and a hat
she loved. Personal eulogies were written and read
aloud by family members and friends. Others in attendance were invited to share their memories of the
deceased. Her favorite music was played. One piece
was the Christmas carol, "Silent Night," even though
the funeral was in the middle of summer. This was
followed by an informal tea and a receiving line of
relatives which allowed those in attendance to express
their condolences and offer support.

An artist friend who had been in precarious health
planned for a party to be held at his home several weeks

after his death. Close friends were invited, and his favorite foods were served. Photos of his work and art projects were displayed. His personality seemed to be present. The event became a celebration of the creativity and beauty he had brought to the world as much as an occasion to mourn his loss.

In contrast, I went to a funeral where family members were segregated in a small room during the brief ceremony at the funeral parlor, then whisked off to the graveyard alone. As a result, they missed the opportunity to receive support from those who made the effort to come and be with them.

Children Need to Mourn

One of the worst things we can do is to prevent children from being involved in the death rituals of funeral and burial and the pain associated with death.

In the past when most children were raised on farms, death was a regular occurrence. Animals were slaughtered for food, or were sometimes attacked and killed by other animals, or baby animals died. Birth and death were taken in stride, not always without hurt, pain and grief, but as natural experiences. Children witnessed these events and learned to accept them as a normal, not frightening, part of life.

Today's child, raised in the city away from the natural reality of death, may be totally unprepared to cope with the death of a parent or a grandparent. Whenever children are exposed to death, every opportunity should be taken to talk frankly about what death means and how they feel about it. Ideally, the first time would be the funeral of a distant relative or acquaintance. Children should be encouraged to examine and talk about their feelings.

Open discussion about the possibility of the death of any family member should be an ongoing process. All questions should be answered sincerely and honestly. Options about disposal of the body should be discussed such as donating organs for transplant, and preferences for burial or cremation. Children should be involved in plans about special music, flowers, or substitute donations to research organizations like the heart fund or cancer research, a children's home or a drug rehabilitation program.

Putting Affairs in Order

Financial matters should be worked out in advance to cover the death of one or both spouses. Plans should be made for the guardianship of minors. Children should be included in such family conversations as soon as they are able to understand the information. Wills should be made and reviewed regularly. A special file should be kept on insurance benefits, pension plans, Social Security, and investments. At least once a year this information should be discussed and reviewed, and the file should be revised when necessary.

Death may still be the last taboo in our country, but for grieving survivors the chores of sorting through the chaos of business papers, money worries, estate taxes, and possibly having to sell the family home and move, can be the cruelest legacy you leave behind.

To put off taking care of these matters is to deny the reality of death. You cannot do the grieving for your loved ones, but you can spare them some of the anger and frustrations about money and financial survival that follow your death. This applies to both women and men, parents and adult children. Inform yourself about these matters now while you can still do something about them.

Offering Comfort

Grieving doesn't end with the funeral. It has barely begun. Mourning is intensely personal. No two people grieve alike. During the weeks and months after a loss, some survivors will express deep emotions by crying; others will quietly reflect.

In offering support and comfort to a friend or relative who is grieving, it is important to avoid platitudes and trite sayings. Don't give advice or explanations. Death is a mystery.

No one understands why death occurs or the timing of death. Trying to explain only interferes with the pain of the bereaved, especially if the explanation sounds superficial and insincere.

The best way to offer support to friends is to let them know that you are there, perhaps hold their hands and listen. Listen actively. Don't relate your experiences. Be there with them—be there for them. It is always appreciated when you bring food or drinks, or run errands. (See Appendix A.)

It takes a lot of love and sensitivity to allow your friend to express grief in the way that is most helpful to her. Just remember that it is crucial for her to express grief. Suppressing her feelings will only lead to physical and emotional problems later.

Understanding Your Own Grief

When someone you love dies and you don't feel normal, you may wonder what is wrong with you. There is nothing wrong with you. Part of what is wrong is our current social attitude about death and dying.

Cultural influences are subtle, but powerful. Today people do not know what to expect while mourning. They wonder, what is normal? How long will it go on? Will I ever feel a joy for living again?

Yes, you *will* return to a "normal" life, a complete life of your own, in time. It won't happen the day after the funeral. The more close and complex your relationship with the person who died, the more painful and involved and lengthy will be the process of letting go.

Saying goodbye takes time. It's important to understand the steps in the process, the conflicting emotions you may feel, and to know that you're working out your grief in the way that's necessary for you.

CHAPTER TWO

STAGES OF GRIEF

We are all different. Each person is an accumulation of genetic material, culture, family backgrounds, personal experiences, and unique coping styles. So when we experience the death of a loved and treasured person, we react in slightly different ways based on these factors. Each of us is unique, a composite of multiple influences.

Yet grieving follows a predictable pattern—while each of us goes through the steps in that pattern in our own way, it helps to know that our feelings are understood by others.

This book is written with the hope that when you or someone you know has lost a special person you will have some idea of what to expect during the time of grief and mourning. And to let you know that in time you will recover and begin again to feel a joy in living.

A loss of someone in death is a wound, and as with any injury, illness, or physical wound, you must allow yourself time to heal. The psychological pain that you will feel is just as important as any observable physical wound. Time gives you distance from the events of the death and the personal relationship that you had with that person. Time alone will not heal you, but the timing

of the grieving process will help you to become whole
again if you allow yourself to experience and feel what
you must to release the deceased and to get on with
your own life.

Traditionally, the official time of mourning has been
one year. This is common in many cultures and reli-
gions. Judaism, for example, organizes the mourning
year into four sections—three days of deep grief, seven
days of mourning, thirty days of gradual adjustment,
and eleven months of readjustment for remembrance
and healing.

Often one year is not enough time. In the loss of a
spouse or child, for instance, two years may be a more
realistic expectation of the time needed to heal and
recover. If the grieving process is allowed to run its
natural course there is a typical time frame that you can
anticipate.

The steps are as follows:

      Stage I   –Breaking Old Habits
                  Time of death to eight weeks

      Stage II   –Beginnings of Reconstruction of Life
                  Eight weeks to one year

      Stage III   –Seeking New Love Objects or Friends
                  One year to two years

      Stage IV   –Readjustment Completed
                  After two years

These times are not rigid, but rather a flexible guide-
line of what is generally reported by persons who have
gone through a grieving process. Much depends, of
course, on the degree of intimacy you have had with the
person who died. If it was a spouse or child with whom
you were living, then it is a more profound experience
than if you didn't live with the person. For instance, if

you lose someone you did not live with, he may be on your mind a lot, but you will not be in the habit of expecting him to come home to supper. You won't have that daily reminder of his absence.

Another important factor is your prior knowledge of the coming loss. If there was a long, serious illness and you had a chance to begin your grieving before the death, you may move through the stages of grief faster.

Let's examine in more detail these stages of present and future adjustments that are necessary to move through grief to a renewed life.

Stage I: Breaking Old Habits
(Death to eight weeks)

The weeks immediately following a death are a time of numbness and confusion. Nothing is normal. Feelings of shock, disbelief, protest, and denial are rampant. Death is a forced separation, a tearing apart. You feel severed and raw, your emotions scattered to the wind. If the death was sudden and unexpected, the anguish is more acute. You may feel an actual physical shock when you first get the news.

Your life is changed from the instant you are told about the death. You feel helpless and powerless to control the events of your life. At the same time you are swept along in a rapid tide of activity. Responsibilities must be met and decisions must be made. Notifying relatives and friends, funeral arrangements, newspaper notices, death certificates, and a myriad of other details demand your attention.

Often the activity is a blessing in disguise. You are involved in the final act of giving or paying tribute to your loved one. The busyness helps you through the first few days, giving you a chance to begin to realize the reality of your loss. But you are extremely vulnerable now and need to protect yourself at all levels.

Habits and Patterns

As the confusion clears a little, you begin to be more aware of the need to adjust to letting go of the habit patterns in the relationship. When people live together, lots of habits are formed. Small ways of interacting are often taken for granted. Things such as expecting your spouse to bring the newspaper into the house, telephoning your mate at a certain time each day, seeing the towels left on the bathroom floor, sleeping on one side of the bed, sitting at a certain place at meals—these are second nature. When these routine situations are interrupted, you must reprogram your expectations at the emotional, physical, and psychic levels. Daily there are little reminders that the fabric of your life has been torn. You feel deep sadness, deprivation, and loss.

Leslie, a teacher, had a habit of making mental notes of events on her job each day to tell her husband about in the evening. After his death she would catch herself thinking of telling him about something and realize with a start that such sharing would not happen. At first the tears came in torrents with the realization. Her feelings of self-pity, loneliness, and helplessness were overwhelming. But gradually, slowly, she came to accept his death and stop anticipating their old behavior patterns. Now eight months later, she hardly ever thinks of him in that context. She shares her stories with other teachers or occasionally with friends.

As the reality of the loss is accepted, the futility of anticipating former routine events is realized, and in time, changes in life-style are recognized and eventually appreciated. Gradually, loneliness changes to enjoying time alone to think or to be creative, to begin or finish projects long waiting for attention.

During this early time a grieving person may experience changes in everyday living, such as eating and sleeping habits. Sleep is often restless and may include disturbing dreams, waking in the middle of the night and not being able to go back to sleep, or waking at 5 A.M. exhausted and tense. Some people eat more when they are feeling deprived as a way to nurture themselves. Other people eat less, lose their appetites completely and stop cooking meals. Food loses taste for most people. These disturbances last only a short time and clear up naturally. If they persist for many weeks, you may want to make an effort to change them, or to seek counseling to talk about your progress or where you are stuck.

The Deceased's Presence

Tears and feelings of profound sadness come up at unexpected times. You may be watching a movie or television program, or driving a car, shopping for groceries, sitting in church, playing tennis; any time that thoughts of the dead person arise is a potential time for tears. It is very important to let those feelings of sadness out. It is cleansing, purifying. Allow yourself to experience the tears and you will recover more quickly. Stopping yourself from crying serves no function, and letting the tears flow will bring some release of pain.

In the early weeks of grieving it is common and normal to be preoccupied—even obsessed—with the dead person. In fact, you may feel disloyal if you do not have her on your mind constantly.

Talking to your deceased child or spouse or parent is one way to release stress. Going to the grave, writing letters to her, keeping a journal, or having an imaginary conversation are all ways to complete the unfinished business in the relationship. It is irrelevant whether the deceased hears the messages or not; like funerals, it's for *you*.

There are always things left unsaid, business unfinished, when someone dies. By continuing to communicate to your dead loved one, you can complete the relationship. Many people report a sensing or feeling of the presence of the deceased around them. These experiences are neither strange or abnormal; they can be a great comfort to the survivor and in time will be less important.

Marty recently told me that he knew his dead wife was "around" and that if she could talk, she would give him hell for buying a new car. After making joint decisions for years, it is only natural that he would know how his former mate would respond to his choices. Marty continued to consider her probable reactions as he shopped for a car, even though she had been dead for almost a year. In his thoughts, he had conversations with her to satisfy himself.

Marty's "talks" with his late wife were a way of continuing to include her in his life, acknowledging her importance to him. Old patterns take time to break. By the time Marty buys his next car, her input will be less important to him.

Go Easy on Yourself

Children, pets, aging parents, job stresses and any other demands must be put in the background as much as possible during this early grieving period. Mental confusion and low energy levels are very common. Fatigue and exhaustion result from both expending energy to cope and resisting the emotional responses that continue to surface. This is not a good time to make any major decisions.

The simplest habits of daily living such as shopping, eating, sleeping or dressing may become burdensome for a while. But every day you survive takes you farther along the path to recovery.

Stage II: Beginning to Reconstruct Your Life
(Eight weeks to one year)

Even after a few months have passed, your pain and confusion are still acute. But they gradually diminish, and recovery begins to take place automatically and without conscious awareness. You are healing. Habit patterns will still be erratic and in a state of flux, changing from the former established routines.

Sally's husband loved romaine lettuce. She didn't like it, but automatically continued to buy it when she shopped for groceries. She would take it home, wash it and store it in the refrigerator until it spoiled and she had to throw it out. After three months, it finally dawned on her that she didn't have to buy romaine lettuce anymore. Small changes like this reduce the denial of death and let reality slowly creep in.

Eating and sleeping patterns are still unsettled during this second phase. Eating more or less than usual, or not wanting to take time to prepare meals or really taste food, are typical behaviors at this time.

Sleeping may still be a problem. You may wake up in the night restless and tense. You might find yourself unable to completely relax and may worry about feeling constant fatigue.

Working on Your Recovery

During this stage, you will probably have periods of depression, feeling powerless to change the events of your life. Along with the sadness may come periods of low energy and fatigue.

Physical tension and stress will continue. Some survivors try masking the helplessness and distress by using increasing amounts of alcohol, drugs, cigarettes, coffee, or other substances. Behaviors that were social and moderate in the past may become temporarily or permanently excessive. The danger with this type of coping is that if the grieving process is blocked by artificial methods, a dependency may result.

Occasional use need not be of concern, but if you begin to depend on these substances to get through the day or night, take a good look at what you are really doing to yourself, and what you are trying to avoid. Resistance to feeling and dealing with emotional pain is the biggest danger you face right now.

Get help if you need it. We all need help sometime in our lives. Seeking counseling no longer has the social stigma it used to have. Recovering from any major loss in life can be speeded up and made less difficult with professional assistance. So if you feel bogged down or stuck, go get some help, whether it takes one visit or several until you feel better able to cope on your own.

Overall health may be of concern. You may be physically run down and more vulnerable and susceptible to minor illnesses like viruses, sinusitis or flus. Major sickness can easily occur now, especially illnesses that are directly stress-related, such as colitis or digestive tract disorders like gastritis and ulcers. Blood pressure changes can occur; even heart diseases or cancer may show up.

Accidents are more likely to happen during periods of extreme stress. We are all more prone to accidents when suffering from emotional stress and unresolved feelings. Take extra precaution when driving, hiking, or engaging in other activities.

It is very important to be as gently to yourself as possible and to avoid adding any more stressful situations to your life for a while. Try to eat well, get the best sleep that you can, exercise regularly, and allow yourself to feel and experience any emotions that may arise. Cry when you need to. Seeds for chronic illnesses can be planted under the tension of the grieving process and may pop out several years later if your emotions are denied or repressed.

Emotional disturbances continue to require a great deal of energy for the first year. Spontaneous crying at unexpected times and places can be both a surprise and sometimes embarrassing. Seeing a happy family or watching a romantic scene on television or a movie often strike a sentimental nerve and rekindle feelings of loss and deprivation. Tears flow and wash away more of the pain. It's okay—in fact, it's helpful—to feel sad and cry. It's cleansing, healing.

Worry and feeling helpless are common early in the grieving process and are normal aspects of the depression experienced in grief. Concern about being able to take care of yourself, of meeting basic survival needs, of having the energy to get through another day may surface from time to time. Thinking that the present feelings may never end contributes to self-pity and helplessness. These feelings are normal and in time will pass.

Memory lapses are also common now. Marge told me that she misplaced the settlement check from her late husband's life insurance policy. It was missing for weeks, as she searched everywhere. She felt stupid to have lost something so important to her survival. Finally, she looked through a box of scrap papers that she was about to throw away and she found the check which she had unconsciously thrown out. Another subconscious form of denial? Probably. And in her state of mental confusion, carelessness.

Thoughts of suicide may surface from time to time. These are normal and common. If, however, they become obsessive and linger in your mind, get some professional help. Being dead yourself may look like an easy way out of your misery. It isn't. It's a cop-out. And those who love you and depend on you would be left with a double whammy of dealing with two deaths.

Suicide during grief is the ultimate in self-pity and helplessness, not a solution to anything. So when such thoughts come up, notice them and let them pass. There's no need to dwell on them or wallow in them or worry about them. Let them go and get on with your life. Your life is necessary and important and unique and valuable.

Dwelling on the circumstances of the death and negative parts of the relationship will only delay your recovery time. You may think frequently about your mistakes or the things you didn't do, and now wish you had. Whatever happened between you, you did the best you could at the time. Continually going over situations cannot change them. Forgive yourself—if there is anything to forgive that is still unfinished. Forgive your spouse or parent or child for anything left unresolved or unsaid. Begin to think in positive terms of the good times in the relationship and give up the painful ones. Above all, stop punishing yourself!

Dreams, daydreams, and fantasies are a clue of how you are doing as you progress through the first year. Dreams of the dead person are part of processing and letting go. A dream log can be very helpful and valuable if you need to seek counseling at some time. You can keep track of the progression of your dreams by writing about each one in a notebook. Record them as soon as you wake up. If you have trouble remembering your dreams at first, just suggest to yourself as you begin to fall asleep that you want to remember your dreams, and you will soon begin to remember them. Record as much detail as possible; include the setting, time of the day or night, colors, people, how you feel, vehicles, water, animals, and other details. Dreams recorded over a period of time reveal more information than a single dream.

Betsy had a series of dreams about water. Water for her was symbolic of the flow of her life. In her early dreams, shortly after her husband's death, she was in a boat that was about to turn over, and she was struggling not to fall into the water, which was cold and frightening. Later dreams revealed the water to be less deep, but still cold and dark. Gradually over a year, the water in her dreams became warmer and clearer, and in the last recorded water dream, she was playing and swimming in it. She was ready to get back in the swim of life!

Special Times

Holidays and family celebrations will be very hard the first year. Birthdays, Christmas, and other sentimental holidays are the worst ones without the one you've lost. But it gets easier each time. Try to have those you love best and who are most supportive around you for these occasions. You may feel prepared to "get through" these times and try to steel yourself against the inevitable hurt. You're not steel—you are human. Even though these special days will be hard and painful, you can stand it.

Allow yourself to feel sadness, disappointment, resentment, anger, or any other emotion that comes up. To feel nothing—just a kind of numbness—is okay as long as it's not a way of blocking emotions. You will experience your emotions when you are ready to. I encourage you not to block the emotions when they surface. Experience them, feel them, then put them behind you.

Sheila, a young widow, thought she was all ready for her first holiday season after her husband's death. At a big family Thanksgiving dinner, she wouldn't allow herself to feel sad. She was pleased that it was so easy. She had worried that she would have feelings of sadness and pain, and made every effort to enjoy herself and not feel depressed. Three days later, she went to visit relatives in another city. Sheila spent the entire visit sick in bed with severe pains in her stomach and back. This physical breakdown was her way of coping with the emotional pain that she repressed on Thanksgiving day. Instead of letting the feelings out, she fought them, turned them inward, and later got sick.

Next year it should be much easier for Sheila. By the second year, new family rituals will begin to be established and her dead husband will be missed less.

Another difficult date is the anniversary of the death. This is especially hard if the death occurred around a holiday or someone's birthday. Remember, each year it gets easier to handle. You will survive! You will grow with new areas of strength and courage in your life that you never realized you had. Make a conscious choice toward life and accept the pain that is part of it.

Rediscovering Yourself

Searching for and establishing a new and separate personal identity is a major part of this second stage of recovery. It is a slow process that can be both painful and joyous. You may still feel married, or still feel you have a best friend, even though she's gone. If your child has died, you may feel that your life has no meaning. You miss him terribly!

Some people, in coping with a major loss, immerse themselves in a flurry of activity. Many get wholeheartedly involved in outside activities, in work, finding a new job, or returning to school. There can be a "driven" aspect to this—a compulsion to "throw" yourself into something and always be busy so you won't have to think about or feel the pain. This is another form of the denial process, a way to avoid the work of grieving.

If you feel that your relationship with the deceased somehow involved personal failure on your part, then it seems all the more important to prove your worth, especially to yourself. Staying busy is a way to try to fill your mind with other information, pressures, and demands so that you will not have to think about your emotional state. You hope that involvement in external events will make the internal pain disappear. Unfortunately, it doesn't work! You will have to complete your grieving process or eventually suffer the consequences. Face the guilt feelings so you can put them behind you for good. Forgive yourself and let it go.

If you're not using activity to dull your emotions, begin to search for your special skills, interests and ways to grow and to support yourself. Many people have found returning to school both rewarding and a good way to make new friends, especially for widows. Begin to set positive goals for yourself.

Vocational or job training is another option. One young widow I know enrolled in a special school to become a travel agent. She plans to use her insurance settlement to buy or start her own travel agency.

Moving to another home or city may be tempting during this first year. It is better to avoid doing this if possible. Most often such moves are impulsive and later regretted.

By the anniversary of the death, you will be aware that you are somewhat better and renewed. You have a way to go, but you have accepted your loss and are beginning to plan your future.

Stage III: Seeking New Love Objects or Friends (12 months to 24 months)

Life has returned to "normal." Some former habits are firmly re-established and new habits have become routine. Daily tasks are automatic. Emotional pain is less acute.

Your loved one is not in your thoughts as often.

Mourning may continue as a ritual, but the intensity has greatly diminished and will not be as devastating as earlier. You will seldom cry in public, although there will still be moments of sadness and depression. Depression is an outer manifestation of an internal struggle. The internal struggle throughout the entire mourning process is to come to terms with the reality of your loss and to find a new identity and rebuild your life.

Renewed Health

After the first year, eating and sleeping habits should have returned to normal. Laughter, fun, happiness, and a sense of humor are returning. Smoking, using alcohol and drugs return to the pre-loss patterns in the second year. Memory is normal again.

Health usually returns to normal or may be better than before, provided that the emotional issues and pain of the bereavement have been dealt with and released.

You'll experience heavy emotional reactions less and less often. Anger, resentment, guilt, anxiety, and fears of being able to survive on your own should be part of the past now, or rapidly fading away. Dreams will have lighter content and portray a mood of involvement in life.

Friends

You should have made new friends, some of whom will have had similar experiences. Start planning interesting leisure time activities with new people or dear old friends. Maybe a trip, a new recreational activity, political action, volunteer work, classes, learning a language, whatever you want to do. Get involved.

If you are working, you will be better at managing your time and responsibilities. All members of the family will begin to come to terms with your new relationships and changes in the family adjusting to the absence of the dead person.

One day you will wake up and know that the healing process has been working. You realize that your thinking is sharper and clearer, that your judgment and perceptions are more rational and reliable, that your emotions have settled down and you are less preoccupied with yourself. Overall, you feel more alive and happy. You made it!

Stage IV: Readjustment Completed
(After the second year)

This final stage is characterized by the end of mourning. Routine habits of life have blended, old patterns and new patterns come together and are carried out without conscious thought. You are living your new life.

Living space, working arrangements, child care, leisure time activities, dating and other friendships and relationships have pretty well settled into a comfortable flow. Life is less fragmented and hectic. You will be less "self" occupied and more "other" occupied. You have a new life and a new philosophy.

There will be times of euphoria and contentment. The future will seem bright. You will feel stronger than ever, and you will know now that you can survive any loss. You may not want to, but you know that you can. Now you know that pain passes in time, and the growth you make can be personally very rewarding.

Overall, your new life has become normal for you. You feel that you are a different person, and in many ways you are. If you have used the time of mourning to slowly heal and have allowed yourself to experience and express the deep and often painful emotions that have been brought to the surface in your grieving, you will now be ready for the next chapter of your life. Welcome it and enjoy the strength you now have to face new challenges that await you. Welcome back to the world of the living and the loving.

CHAPTER THREE

FEELINGS OF GRIEF

The feelings of grief last far longer than society in general allows. Even closest friends may expect us to be back to "normal" in a few weeks after a death. But living with loss is not so simple. The death of someone close may cause emotional pain and confusion for months or even years. Losing someone we love through death is one of the most traumatic of life's experiences. Acute grief affects several million people every year. And it occurs to every one of us at some time in our lives. Several times if we live a long life. People we love die and we mourn their loss.

Almost two million people die every year in the United States—and nearly every one of them leaves behind someone who mourns for their loss.

Other changes cause grief: there are over one million divorces per year; thousands more people separate from spouses. Children, relatives, and friends suffer from the turmoil and confusion of losing a valuable relationship. People leave careers, have accidents, grow older. All significant life changes involve a grieving process as we say goodbye to part of the old self, old ways, familiar paths.

Being able to manage grief is important for both the

individual experiencing a loss, and for the society of which he or she is part. Management of grief means handling it—understanding your feelings, living with the loss and change, fitting the events of a death or change and its aftermath into your life, so that *you* can go on living.

The stresses of unsuccessful, uncompleted grieving can lead to serious physical illness, lost hours from a job, mental distress, and even death.

As traumatic and difficult as it can be, loss is not rare. It is universal. No one in the world escapes some time in life when he he or she must come to terms with a loss through death, illness, separation or other dramatic change. The process of grieving is also universal, and it is subject to cultural influences such as the rituals of death and burial. The prevailing social attitudes dictate how emotions are expressed.

The grief process as most people experience it has been broken down into five identifiable stages by Dr. Elisabeth Kubler-Ross, a psychiatrist who worked with patients who had terminal illnesses. She discovered that most patients experienced periods of denial, anger, bargaining, and depression before reaching acceptance. These feelings, usually in the order that Kubler-Ross identified, are common to all of us when we are faced with adjusting to changes in our lives, both positive and negative changes.

Thanks to the pioneering work of Dr. Kubler-Ross, we can help people know what to expect when tragedy strikes in our lives. However, we are all unique personalities. Not everyone moves through these stages in the same way with the same timing. Some people get stuck in one stage or another and never move on to the final stage of acceptance and of rebuilding their lives. Others experience the feelings more than once, perhaps reaching depression, then going back to denial or anger.

Let's look at the five stages.

Denial

The shock of finding out that someone died is felt by some people as a physical jolt. A state of numbness and disbelief takes hold. This is a protective state which insulates the bereaved from the anguish that will follow in the coming months in coming to terms with the death. The denial stage usually lasts from four to six weeks. Sometimes a person feels guilty during this time because she doesn't "feel" anything. She may not cry at the funeral, or she may take care of others who are expressing their grief. This is normal. You do not need to force yourself to feel something that is not natural for you, but don't hold back your feelings either as they start to surface. After about six weeks if a person is stoically fighting his grief and strong feelings, or is still feeling numb, he is denying his feelings and is headed for emotional trouble.

The benefit of the time of denial is to mobilize your inner resources to allow you to face the reality of your new situation. As you collect yourself it is time to begin looking at what has happened and to acknowledge other feelings.

Anger

Anger may be expressed outwardly as rage, or turned inward and be experienced as depression. But underneath all anger is fear. Fear of meeting your own needs, of making decisions, fear that you won't be able to manage financial, emotional, and physical survival.

When anger is expressed outwardly, a person may project it on other people. She may be angry at the doctor for not giving adequate care, or at the policeman who was insensitive when he told her of the death. He may be furious at her mother for telling him what to do with the children during the funeral. They may be angry with God, for the injustice and unfairness of the death. Blaming others is a way of avoiding the personal pain and sorrow and despair of coming to terms with the fact that your life goes on without the dead person.

The danger for a person who projects her anger onto others is that she may become caught up in bitterness, resentment, and alienation. As young children we are taught by well-meaning parents that to express anger is wrong, it is not nice, it is unbecoming, so we learn to stuff our feelings insides. We learn to deny any feelings *like* anger such as irritation, resentment, frustration, disappointment, terror, fear, hurt. We love and need our parents; we want their approval, so we do as we are told and we deny and hide our feelings.

Unfortunately, we must learn to reverse this process later in our lives. The death of a loved one is a time of testing emotionally. Our emotions are part of us and by acknowledging and owning them we can reach new levels of sensitivity, love, and self-awareness.

First admit your anger. You'll find that you aren't simply angry at the doctor—you may also be angry at the husband or parent who died and left you. Many people tell me, "How can I be angry at my child? She didn't want to die." Of course not, but you may feel angry at losing her, at the strong feelings you now feel, at the financial aspects. There may not be a real target for your anger; sometimes life is unfair. We all have different reasons for feeling what we feel. Your feelings are legitimately part of you; don't be ashamed of them. Hiding your anger won't make it disappear. You'll get past it more quickly if you bring it out into the open.

After you admit your anger to yourself, report it to someone you trust. This may be frightening to you, but anger accumulates and will erupt eventually, maybe frightening or hurting another person. A good friend or a professional counselor will help you work through your feelings of anger or fear. Learning to recognize and deal with milder emotions when they arise is the best way to avoid explosive out-of-control outbursts of anger turned to rage.

Begin to notice when you feel irritated, hurt or disappointed. As you start to handle these emotions at the time they occur, you will notice that your anger is in much more control.

When anger does build up to the point of explosion, there are techniques that you can use to let off the steam without hurting yourself or other people. Because pent-up emotions are stored in the body, one way to release them is through physical activity. Screaming or beating on a pillow or tearing up a telephone book can be helpful. Take a long walk, chop wood, or work out in a gym. Go swimming or take up a physical activity you enjoyed in the past. Get involved with such an activity on a regular basis for a while. Concentrate on your body, not your grief.

If you scream or beat on a pillow, you will get some immediate and temporary relief. Find a private place alone and shout or talk out your present frustrations. This is helpful but only a temporary solution to let off steam. Plan a longer-term program to continue to get into contact with your feelings and handle them. Getting counseling and/or joining a group with other people who have had a similar death in their family is an excellent idea.

Finally, turn the energy of your anger into doing something positive. Start a self-help group for others who had a similar death in their families: for instance, begin a program to train ambulance drivers or police officers to be more sensitive to the dying. One woman whose daughter was killed by a car driven by a drunken driver started MADD (Mothers Against Drunken Drivers). The organization has spread all over the country and influenced legislation to curb driving while intoxicated. (See Appendix B.)

Bargaining

Bargaining before the death occurs may be wishing that a new cure will miraculously be found, or wanting to live until after Christmas or Hanukkah, or making deals with God that the disease is misdiagnosed. Bargaining goes on in our minds to help buy time to accept the truth of the situation.

After the death, bargaining is less important. You soon realize that fantasies of trying to bring the person back to life are unrealistic. They only delay the necessary responsibility to emotionally release the loved one who died. Eventually as you begin to make new friends and involve yourself in new activities, you will live less in the past, and your dreams of how it could have been will fade.

Depression

Depression is often defined as anger turned inward. It includes feelings of helplessness, hopelessness, and powerlessness. Depression is a mood disturbance. Other feelings are sadness, disappointment, and/or loneliness. When a person is depressed, he often withdraws from people and activities, loses capacity for pleasure and avoids the enjoyable activities formerly experienced in life. You may notice physical discomforts such as aches, pains, fatigue, poor digestion, and sleep disturbances. Moderate depression is normal after someone dies. For a while you may want to be alone to sort out your feelings and to begin to make plans for the future. But if your symptoms are severe and lasting, so that you completely lose interest in the outside world, then get professional help. You may find for a while that one day you feel pretty good and the next day you awake with a sense of doom and gloom. This is okay for a while; in time the days of feeling good will outnumber the bad days.

To help yourself during this time, take care of the things that need your attention. Don't put off handling financial and other matters or they will accumulate and overwhelm you later. Ask for comfort and help when you want it. Try to do something special for yourself each day, something that you really like. Take a hot bubble bath, treat yourself to an ice cream cone, listen to music, read for an hour, or whatever is enjoyable to you. Exercise and a good diet will relieve some of your depression.

Some people get stuck in depression. It is important not to resist your feelings or wallow in them. Do something physically active which will help you to sleep better. While you are walking, running, swimming, or playing tennis, concentrate on your body, not on your sadness. Listening to cassette tapes on relaxation, soothing environmental sounds or music are very helpful in reducing your stress and depression.

Guilt

Guilt comes from something we did or said that we wish that he had not done; or from something that we think that we should have said or done that we didn't do. Whenever you find yourself saying *should* or *ought*, you are putting yourself in a position to feel guilt. You may have legitimately and purposely avoided, neglected, injured or damaged another person. If so, then you must take responsibility for your behavior and make amends as well as you can.

On the other hand, you may be creating guilt for yourself unreasonably. If you are saying to yourself or others, "He wouldn't have had the accident if only I hadn't bought him that car," you are creating your guilt by your self-talk. *If only* and *What if* are questions that can never be answered. You do not have the facts available to know what else could have happened. You must rid yourself of the irrational *if only* things you are saying to yourself. These thoughts serve no purpose but to keep you feeling guilty.

Feeling guilt will slow down your recovery. Even if you're convinced that your actions were wrong or insensitive, you must forgive yourself and go on with your life. Feeling guilty over a prolonged time is a choice you are making. You can also choose not to feel guilty. You must accept the reality of what has happened. The death cannot be changed now, but you can change what you think about it. You don't need to become a martyr. No human is perfect—only perfectly human—and that includes making mistakes. Mistakes become valuable when we learn from them. What did you learn from yours?

Interrelationship of Body, Mind and Emotions

Human beings function in life on different levels, the mind or intellect, the emotional or feeling level, and the physical level. The intellectual, reasoning, analytical part is a function of the left hemisphere of our brains. The emotional, feeling, creative part is governed more by the right side of our brains. Our primitive, emotional response to danger and fearful experiences is regulated by our limric brain, a part of our nervous system. When we perceive danger, we react with a fight-or-flight survival response, just as animals do.

At the physical level, our bodies gather information constantly through our five senses, reporting this information about stress level, body temperature, pain, danger and illness through our nervous system to our brains. We process information as thoughts. Our thoughts in turn influence our emotions. All three systems are interrelated and necessary to stay alive. They work together to form a whole balanced system. Holistic health is a philosophy that teaches people to tune into these integral parts of ourselves and to strive to maintain balance.

When one part is ignored, we become out of balance. For example, if you ignore the body's signals to the brain by constant overeating, continuing to smoke when you have a chronic lung disease, or not sleeping when you are exhausted, in time your body will break down. You will become ill and eventually die, perhaps prematurely.

Similarly, a person who ignores or denies strong and painful emotions will eventually break down emotionally, by having anxiety attacks, irrational outbursts of anger, or other neurotic or psychotic symptoms.

This imbalance also happens when a person tries to deal with emotions on an intellectual level, by rationalizing. It doesn't work. Thoughts are thoughts; they cannot be felt. Feelings are feelings; they cannot be thought.

Thoughts, however, affect feelings and the degree of the feelings can be regulated by thoughts. This doesn't mean controlling your emotions by repressing and rationalizing them. It means not letting your negative emotions continue to make you feel bad after such feelings become unproductive. For example, if you use strong words in your thoughts like *terrible*, *never again*, *can't*, or *hate*, then your emotional reactions will be equally strong and may seem overwhelming to resolve. But if you use words like *I choose*, *may*, *examine*, *forgive*, *decided*, then you are making selections and are in control of your emotional choices.

Your thoughts are your self-talk; what goes on inside of your head. You may tune into this talk to take charge of what you're telling yourself. Your self-talk creates your reality. You can use your self-talk to set up emotional barriers, and feel completely helpless and emotionally impotent. Or you can expand your horizons to create positive change and growth.

Acceptance

How will you know when you are well? When you can think of your loved one without strong emotional feelings of longing and sadness. You will remember him or her realistically, neither as an idealized saint nor a villain. You will be living in the present, not stuck in the past, and making plans for the future. You will be able to live with the ambiguity of the never-to-be-answered questions.

You will notice that he or she is in your thoughts less and less as you build your continuing life. You will be able to experience the joys and pleasures that life holds for all of us, alone or with others.

Growing, Renewal

The psychologist Carl Jung said that part of being human involves having problems because human beings have a consciousness, as opposed to lower animals that operate their lives on instincts. Problems force us to a more developed consciousness, a fuller awareness of events and feelings. As Jung says, "Everyone of us gladly turns away from his problems; if possible they must not be mentioned, or better still, their experience is denied. We wish to make our lives simple, certain and smooth. And for that reason problems are taboo. The artful denial of a problem will not produce conviction; on the contrary, a wider and higher consciousness is called for to give us the certainty and clarity we need."

For each death, each survivor feels a different set of reactions and must work through their grieving processes at whatever pace and time is necessary for them. There are similarities among those who manage their grief successfully—and similar blocking patterns for those who have trouble resolving their grief. Focus on your patterns of grieving, monitor your self-talk and emotions to help you raise your consciousness and grow into a stronger, more sensitive person.

CHAPTER FOUR

DEATH OF A SPOUSE

The death of a spouse is a major psychological blow, one of life's biggest losses. Adjusting to and eventually accepting the reality of the death is a long, slow, and painful healing process. We are not prepared to experience the emotional devastation that the death of a husband or a wife brings to us. It takes time to heal the psychological and emotional wound of being widowed. Slowly, little by little, you will heal. You can even grow from your grief. In time you may become more sensitive to the suffering of others, you may find new areas of inner strength and talents within yourself.

When a spouse dies, all the sharing of dreams, the emotional closeness, the years of growth together must now become memories. In a marriage of many years, the two of you have been one in many functional and emotional ways. Now you are without that other half and you may feel incomplete.

If your spouse was relatively young, both of you are cheated of many years of sharing joys, children, goals and growth.

Even if there were many problems in the marriage, you will miss the other person's presence. And now you can no longer try to solve those problems and strengthen the relationship.

The loss of someone as fundamentally intimately important as your wife or husband will hurt deeply. And it will hurt for a long time.

When a loved one dies, there is no hope of reconciliation. Death is irreversible. Death is final—and to accept this reality is one of the most difficult and painful adjustments you will make in your lifetime.

The word *widow* means empty, without a mate. Many cultures have traditional rituals and customs associated with widowhood—recognizing the tragedy of losing a mate in death. But in the United States we have fewer specific norms or cultural guidelines for going through the stages of grief. In fact, we often seem to try to hide widowed persons away. Much of our society is couple-oriented, and couples don't know how a widow or widower fits in. Widows and widowers remind others of the fragile thread of their own relationships. So in a short time the grieving spouse is dropped from social lists and becomes invisible to former friends and associates, especially if former couple friends were through the husband's associates in social clubs or work. You'll find that you must experience most of your grief alone.

Death is part of life, just as love is. Losing a mate may be the price we pay for love. We always take a risk when we involve ourselves in a relationship because losing the loved one will be a trauma. The more intense the love and involvement, the greater the loss.

Your pain in bereavement is unique to you. Your relationship is unique to you. The circumstances of the death are special and unique to you. I will not presume to tell you how or when you will experience your grief. What I can do is to give you broad guidelines that may be helpful.

The Time Frame

If you knew that your spouse had a terminal illness and would die at some time in the near future, you may have begun to prepare yourself psychologically for the death. However, not everyone is realistic about facing such a reality. Some people continue to carry false hope in their hearts until the very end. Their resistance may add to their pain. Knowing ahead of time is like a gift of time if it is used to begin the grieving process, to begin to anticipate what life will be like without your mate.

You may even have had some mixed feelings before your spouse died. Watching a loved one suffer and feeling so helpless after all medical strategies have failed are extremely emotionally draining experiences. You may have wished that the end would hurry to relieve the suffering, yet at the same time felt anxious and fearful of losing your spouse. You may even have felt angry at the extra emotional and physical demands put upon you. Confused and conflicting feelings are normal at a time like this.

No matter how you used your warning time before the death, you will experience shock and disbelief when the death finally happens. The benefits of advance knowledge come later in the grieving process when you begin to pick up the threads of your life. The extended time of grieving should be shorter and less severe.

If you had no prior warning and the death was unexpected, the initial period of shock and disbelief usually lasts longer. There are more pieces of the relationship left hanging and incomplete. It takes longer to sort out your thoughts and feelings.

You will be in an acute grief reaction from the time of the death until about the end of one year. Your healing will be a slow and gradual process, small, progressive steps to begin to know that you will survive on your own. Some of the wounds of the past must heal before you can move into the future.

The second year is a time when you will begin to form new friendships, make changes, set goals and formulate plans involving your future. You will be more emotionally able to let go of your past.

Protect Yourself

During the first months, try to avoid making major demands on yourself. Don't try to sort out all your feelings or plan your future. Take one day at a time. Moving, changing jobs and promotions are all stressful enough anyway. Adding any of these to the natural tension of early grief can bring about a dangerous overload on your psyche. So it's best not to make major changes in your work or residence during the first several months of widowhood.

During the first few weeks, a lot of time and energy will be required to handle practical matters following the funeral, such as autopsy, coroner's reports, insurance company dealings, social security, bank accounts, charge accounts, probate court, and similar business matters.

Other problems connected with everyday living may arise, such as getting the car serviced and repaired, keeping appliances running, getting the lawn cut, changing the name of the responsible party on utility bills, and doing the income tax. They may all sound insignificant, but such chores can seem overwhelming during this period of grieving. These activities help you get on with your own life, but if the tasks seem overwhelming, ask for help from other members of the family, friends, or by hiring someone to take care of some of the demands.

Satisfaction with your life will be at a low point for a while. This is a time to coast. It's not a time to set goals, make any major decisions, or exercise choices that will have long-range effects. It is a time when you may feel a lot of confusion and a little craziness. Let the feelings happen. They will pass.

The confusion you feel is part of the natural healing process. Resistance will only prolong problems, so just let the reactions flow and soon you will evolve into the next stage of recovery. Be patient. The movement is gradual but you *are* moving. You are getting ready to rebuild your life.

During this early part of your recovery you are adjusting to a state of acute emotional deprivation. This is a time to conserve your energy, reduce your frustrations, be patient and gentle with yourself. The pain of your loss will be felt in many large and small ways. Many widowed people report that they continue to sleep on "their" side of the bed and often reach out in sleep for the body of their spouse. Sometimes they awaken to realize with profound sadness the reality of the death. You will probably feel occasional twinges of depression and wishing that things could be the way they were before, but these times will become less frequent as more times passes.

Others in Your Life

Caring for younger children may be a burden during this first year. You may be too exhausted to get up and dress them for school or to make their breakfast. Sometimes you may be short-tempered and impatient. The kids may seem more difficult and more demanding than ever before. They may start acting up at school and at home trying to get your attention and reassurance that you love them and that you will not leave them as their other parent did. They are grieving too. The changes for all of you will be difficult.

Children also mourn each in their own way. They can only absorb and process so much information at a time, so they'll be going through emotional adjustments of their own. They will miss the parent who was primary in their life most. Therefore, a mother who had been at home a lot will be missed more than a father who worked long hours and seldom ate with the family.

Children can also be greatly affected by the behavior of the bereaved parent. It is especially bad for them if the surviving parent becomes withdrawn and unapproachable. They need to talk, cry and work on their personal grief.

Death is the final abandonment. The greatest fear that kids have subconsciously is that they will lose you too. The best thing you can do is to be as honest as possible about what you are experiencing. Children are not stupid; give them credit. Value their love; respect their feelings.

They can be a great source of comfort to you if you let them. They will want to help. Let them do as much as they are capable of doing. Don't shut them out or push them away; you are all in this together. Talk to them, cry with them, share with them your feelings of sadness and pain, and allow them to do the same.

Remember, they are learning from you, and the more open and honest you are, the more permission they will have to be the same way. Let them know that grief is a process, a healing process, and that it will be easier every day and soon you will all be happy and joyful again.

After a year or so you are likely to be more relaxed with the kids, less resentful and angry at having to raise them alone. You will all be much stronger for having to come through this crisis together.

If your children are adults, it is equally important to include them in your grieving process. Don't expect them to automatically know what you want or need. Ask for it. They cannot read your mind. Take responsibility for getting what you want. It can relieve your hurt and emotional pain, and keeps them from trying to guess what you need from them.

Adult children are grieving too. Losing a parent is a

major life event at any age. It is a time when families can come together in a new and wonderfully supportive way. If family communication has been open and caring, mutual support will occur naturally. If not, now is a time to re-establish love and caring for each other, even though your lives may have taken different paths. Don't be afraid to ask for what you need and want.

You can communicate non-verbally by touching. If you want a hug, ask for it. If you don't want to be alone at some particular time, call someone up and ask them to come and stay with you. If you need some time away from your kids, ask a friend or relative to keep them overnight. It is important to ask for what you want. You may not always get what you ask for when you need it. But if you learn to do this and take the risk, you will benefit because you asked. The worst thing that can happen is that you may feel a little rejected and angry.

If you think you need help in communicating better, take a course in assertiveness or effectiveness training. Try your local community college or other adult education classes.

The penalty for not asking for what you want is to become either passive and manipulative, or angry and aggressive. The first is hidden and covert; the second is openly hostile and overt. Neither is effective. Eventually people see through your methods and avoid you.

There is far more pain, hurt, and disappointment in life by being unassertive than by being assertive. There is no doubt—being assertive is risky. You will find out pretty fast who your true friends are, and you may choose to eliminate a few people from your life, but that would happen sooner or later anyway. A true friend is interested in what is best for you and will not abandon you in your time of need. A false friend will flee—and good riddance!

I remember a story that a wise old woman told me years ago. I was a young bride and worried about my house being spic-and-span when visitors came, which was difficult because I worked full-time. She said, "If someone wants to criticize you, they will find a way. Friends come to see *you*—not your house. Enemies come to see your house—not you." It was such a relief to be free of trying so hard to get the approval of others and to just be me.

Sometimes widows lean too heavily on sons or daughters and/or family whom you think will take care of you, like your spouse did. This insecurity is the result of a deep fear and dread of not being able to take care of yourself. It is the deprived-child part in all of us that is dependent and wants the best of what our mother was. We want to be nurtured, loved, supported, and to have all of our basic needs met, especially when we are hurting.

Other people may be willing to provide that kind of care for a while, and spend extra time with you, but they will soon resent your dependence. After a while they will withdraw from you, even avoid you, and you will be forced to come to terms with finding a way to begin to take care of yourself. Occasionally, adult children may be too protective of you. Be aware if this happens and make your independence clear.

After a few months, you will come to full realization that your relationships with relatives and friends have changed. In-laws will become less important (except possibly as grandparents). You may become closer to your own relatives temporarily, until you establish your new priorities and identity. Typically few married friends will continue to be close and intimate with you. This may be a source of some disappointments, regrets and anger.

The best thing to do is to establish new relationships and find new friends as soon as you can. Many communities have programs for widowed people. Check out the one in your town and take time to talk to other folks with similar experiences. Such programs generally have talks by speakers with practical information on legal issues, trust funds, investment possibilities, etc. Some also provide social opportunities to meet other widows or widowers. Some have group counseling and crisis intervention. These groups were started to help people like you. Take advantage of them. Though you may not feel very "social," you'll find that talking with others in similar circumstances helps ease your pain.

Like it or not, this is the time of your life to learn to stand on your own two feet, to learn to become self-sufficient, to become your own person. Anything and everything you can do to discover and maintain your own personal power will make your future life run much more smoothly.

Set New Goals for Yourself

When a year or so has passed, use this time to figure out what it is that you want your life to be like now, six months from now, one year from now, five years from now—then go after it. During this year you will begin to formulate plans for your new life. Jean told me, one year after her husband died suddenly of a heart attack, "I can go where I want, when I want to. I don't have to answer to anyone. For the first time in my life, I am really free. I have no desire to marry again. I like my life just the way it is."

Many women at first prefer the company of other widows, their children, and their grandchildren. By the beginning of the second year after the loss, your expectations are clearer and your interests will be broader. You know what you have to do to survive and will already be doing it. Leisure time activities will be more pleasant. You may travel, play golf or tennis, or go backpacking. You will begin to make plans, to think about the future.

Brady, a widowed friend of sixty-three, discovered backpacking after his wife's death, something he had never done before. Now he hikes with a group of single people every Sunday. He has made new friends, gets exercise, and has discovered some special activities of his own that he did not share with his former spouse. She is not in his thoughts as much as if they had enjoyed backpacking together.

New Abilities

By the second year of widowhood, you won't feel so helpless. You will be more in control of your life. Many people find they have strengths and talents that they never realized they had before. Widowed women, especially those who had never made decisions about business or money, find that they are able to get the information and facts necessary to buy and sell property, invest in the stock market, borrow money, and make other business decisions. People are generally very willing to answer your questions. Don't hesitate to call or visit your banker, lawyer, or insurance agent.

You'll learn to maintain the car, make home repairs, etc., or at least know how to arrange for these services. Make a list of what you need to know and ask all the questions you have until you thoroughly understand. Or go to your public or college library and ask more questions. Read books or take courses that will enlighten you. The more informed you are, the more independent you become. The more you make informed decisions that are in your own best interest, the more control you can exercise over your life. Use others as consultants and resources—but make your own decisions.

Meg is a good example. After studying the market and seeking business advice, she opened a dress shop fourteen months after her husband's death, though she had never worked before. She arranged for a college student to live in and help with her three young children, the housework, and the cooking. Her store is so successful that she is considering opening a second store in a new shopping mall.

Meg says she has never felt so busy and involved and happy. She still thinks of Bill, her dead husband, but he is on her mind less and less. Meg has found new parts of herself that were dormant until she was forced to make decisions on her own about survival for herself and her children. She says that she has learned more about life, herself, and business in the past year than in thirty-eight years she lived before her husband's death. Many widows become interested in a family business and develop strong executive abilities by filling their husband's shoes.

Letting Go

Many widows and widowers continue to wear their wedding rings during the first year of mourning. The ring is a signal to the world that they are not yet ready to pursue other relationships. It is also a form of denial and indication of the continuing emotional connection to the dead spouse. The ring must go eventually—the sooner the better—just as the clothes in the closet and other personal items of the deceased must go.

The ring is a symbolic link with the past. To successfully build a new life, you must relinquish the past. Don't force yourself to take off the ring until you are ready, but pay attention to any emotions that you have connected to the ring. And when you are ready, put it away for good. One widow I know wore the ring on a chain around her neck for a few months after she took it off her finger. Then it went into a safety deposit box to be passed on to her daughter when she was older.

The idyllic image of your former relationship will

slowly fade. Reality gradually emerges and you begin to remember that your spouse had flaws as well as the beautiful and positive parts.

Len's wife was an alcoholic. At first, after she died, he could only remember her as a beautiful woman, the mother of his children. After about ten months, he was willing to admit how relieved he was not to have to put up with her lies about drinking, her unpredictable behavior at home and at business parties, and the terrible arguments that they had when she was drunk. He was even able to express his anger and disappointment in not having a quality of love in the marriage that might have been there if she had not been an alcoholic.

After a year or so, if your spouse is still in your thoughts daily, you are stuck in your grieving process. It is important for you to begin to let go. If you are still holding on, try this exercise. Lie down and relax completely. Imagine that your mate is lying on the floor with you. Try to pick him or her up every time you get up. Carry him/her with you as you cook, shop, work . . . everywhere. You are exhausted. The weight is unbearable . . . you have no strength or energy left for anything or anyone else in your life. Now lay the person down and say goodbye with love and let go. Notice your feelings. If tears come, let them out. Repeat the exercise until the emotions are resolved and you can stand calmly alone.

Another very effective way to complete the unfinished business of the relationship is to write a letter to your spouse. It is a way to finish old feelings and conversations that you carry around in your head. Write a letter to say goodbye. Tell all of your feelings of sadness, frustration, anger, resentment at being left alone. Express love, regret and whatever else you want to tell her.

This letter is for your eyes only unless you choose to share it, though you probably won't. It may take several days to finish it. If feelings come to the surface, allow yourself to experience them. The final purpose of the letter is to release your spouse with love.

Take off the ring. Put away the pictures. Throw away or give away the rest of the clothes. Let go! You will feel much lighter. You'll be free to go on with your own life.

Begin to think of yourself as happy and fulfilled. You are whole. What changes need to be made? Lose weight . . . spruce up the house . . . new clothes? If you would like a new body imagine, improve it. Your body is the only one you get, so it's important to take care of it. Grieving takes a toll on your physical health. The stress of grieving must be short-term or serious chronic disease may set in. If your health is bad and you are still preoccupied with thoughts of your spouse, try professional help.

As time goes on, heavy emotional reactions will be experienced less and less often. Anger, resentment, guilt, anxiety, and fears of not being able to survive on your own will become part of the past now, or rapidly fade away. Dreams will have lighter content and portray a mood of involvement in life.

New Friendships

Some of your new friends will have had similar experiences. Together, you can move into your new lives. Start sharing leisure activities or special interests with new people. Get involved in life.

If you are working, you will be better at managing your time and responsibilities. If you have dependent children at home, they will also begin to come to terms with the changes in the family. You all will probably feel occasional twinges of depression and wish that things could be as they were before, but these times will become fewer and farther between.

Dating

You may have had little interest in dating. But in the second year you may begin seriously searching for a new love. Your relationships will become more authentic, deeper, more open and more trusting. The men or women who interest you now may be quite different from your dead spouse. Earlier you may have been attracted to someone who was similar to him/her in some way. Perhaps a subconscious effort to replace him/her was at work.

Now, after a few years, you have grown and changed, and a different type of person may be more attractive to you. You may feel that if you had a chance to remarry your husband/wife again, you would not do so. After all, the circumstances of the death forced you to change, to get out in the world and become more independent. You are not necessarily attracted to the same type of person. Your attitudes and values are always changing. Being open to new opportunities and new life-styles is what living is all about.

If you become interested in someone or some activity that you know your former spouse would disapprove of, you may have a few minutes of guilt, as if he/she is looking over your shoulder. Forget it. The past is over—past. You are the one responsible for your life now. Let go of that old tape that says *you should* do things in the old way. You are not the *old* you anymore. You are the *new* you and only you can make your own decisions.

Sexuality

Younger widows are more likely to begin to seek sexual activity sooner and more frequently than older people. Sometimes there is a period of promiscuity, of searching for validation and self-worth through sexual encounters. Sometimes there is a strong desire to be physically close, to touch and be touched. Another desire is to psychologically fill the empty spot in your heart and your bed through the intimacy of sexual intercourse. When you are looking for love and only get sex, you may be disappointed and regret the whole adventure. But before long you will try again.

Sexuality and the desire for sexual satisfaction are part of a lifelong pattern. Health and the availability of a willing partner are more important than age. If an active and satisfying sex life with your former partner was important, then it will continue to be a priority.

The absence of a regular sexual partner can cause emotional conflict and physical frustration. Dreams may become sensual in nature, even to the point of being orgasmic. They may even include images of sexual relations with your children or friends, and if this happens there is no need to feel shocked or ashamed. These people generally represent some aspect of the lost relationship, or some area of deprivation in your current situation.

It is a good practice to masturbate, if this is within your personal moral code. Masturbation can have several positive benefits: it is a good way to relieve physiological tension; it is an excellent and fast way to cope with frustration; it is a way to nurture yourself. It may also be the sexual release that can delay or prevent you from becoming involved with someone else before you are ready. Remember, this is a time of extreme vulnerability and it is very easy to make decisions or choices that may not be in your own best interest in the long run. Go slowly and carefully in the beginning.

Sexual frustration alone should not lead you into a new relationship, especially with any hopes for it to last *forever*. Companionship is fine, but be aware of how much you are substituting a new person for your dead mate.

Lisa started dating three months after her husband died. At first she was concerned about being with a new man, afraid that she might not do or say the right things, or even know what would be expected of her. Lisa chose as her first partner a man who "had a beard and looked just like Jim." The relationship was not right for her; it lasted for only a few months. However, it got her through that difficult first encounter with another person of the opposite sex.

Keep in mind, too, that there are unscrupulous people who consider you good prey and for selfish motives want to use you sexually, and/or get money you may inherit. You may yearn for love and support, but it is better to give it to yourself for now, while you are vulnerable.

Remarriage

Older men and women tend to take longer to begin seeking a new mate. Women, especially those who evaluate their chances of remarriage, choose rather than to compete with younger women for the few available men to simply give up any idea of vigorously searching for another mate. Men, on the other hand, almost always remarry within a short period of time. Men flourish with a woman to wait on them and to meet their sexual and other physical needs. Of course, men have more options than women. There are more available females in most age groups. Men or women may choose other options besides marriage, including women who find relationships with younger men.

Many women have told me that although they loved their husbands, they would never marry again and serve the needs of another. One widow put it this way. She said, "I served my time. I raised three children. My husband was a good man. When he died, I was lost for over a year. But now I'm happy. This is my time for me." This is borne out in the time frame for remarriage.

Widows who remarry do so a little after four years on the average, while widowers remarry within two years.

Age is a significant factor in remarriage for a widow. Young women under the age of twenty-four tend to remarry within one year. Some widows report that they do not wish to ever marry again, but many do. The older the woman is when she is widowed, the less her chances of finding a suitable new mate. By age sixty-five, only thirty percent of women are married as opposed to seventy percent of the men. Middle age years are those when many people become widowed. Widows under thirty years have the best opportunity to remarry. The majority of women widowed during the middle years, ages thirty-five to fifty-four, continue to remarry. After fifty-five, there is a major drop in remarriage for women.

After the Second Year

You may have decided to relocate in a new home or town, gone back to school or taken a job. It is likely that you have found a new love or mate by now and/or arranged your sex life in a way that no longer causes conflict. And you have established friendships that are a support system for you. You have friends with whom you can share a dinner, go to a show, or take a trip. Your relationships with your children will be settled down. Your self-esteem is back intact, and life in general is more satisfying.

A former student of mine decided to move to a new town a couple of years after the death of her husband and the accidental death of one of her teen-age sons. In getting ready to leave, she threw a big party to celebrate her survival and to thank the people who had been her friends and supported her through the tragic and painful times. The party was fun and a great ritual to end one phase of her life, and celebrate the transition from the past to the hopeful and exciting future. It was a way to acknowledge and thank her friends, and a tribute for the living.

CHAPTER FIVE

DEATH OF PARENTS

Adults of young to middle age are truly "in the middle" between their older parents and their younger children, and with varying degrees of dependency on both. Generally, some time in mid-life one or both parents die and the adult children become the elders of the family.

The key issues that determine how the death of a parent will affect an adult child are: the nature of the relationship with that parent; the age of the child when the death occurs; the emotional maturity of the surviving child; the length of time of warning prior to the death; and the time the parent and child have spent discussing both the practical and emotional aspects involved in the parent's death.

Obviously, the older and more mature the son or daughter is, the longer the time of warning, the more open the relationship between parent and child, the easier it will be to process the grief for a dead parent. When a young child loses a parent, or the death is sudden, or the relationship is tense—the grief may remain unresolved for years.

The stages of recovery and the processes of grieving after the death of a parent are usually not as disabling or intense as when you lose a spouse, lover, or child.

Parents are expected to die before their children do, so to some extent we're all prepared for our parents to die. Not that it is ever easy to lose a significant emotional relationship, but most of us hold a prevailing notion that it is just or appropriate when death comes to someone who is older and has had a chance to live long enough to complete some or all of the tasks of the life cycle. It's much easier to accept that kind of loss without the sense of rage that comes up when a child or younger adult dies.

Lingering Dependency on Parents

The age of the child when his parent dies influences how well he will handle the grief. For a small child, the death of a parent is a mystery. The child will often have feelings of guilt and think that he caused the death by some "bad" or naughty act. Or he may be possessed by a fear of being abandoned or punished.

Joan lost her mother in a typhoid epidemic when she was five years old. Three weeks later an older brother died of the same disease. Joan was too young to understand death. She only knew that her mother had disappeared. That traumatic loss created in Joan lifelong fears of losing someone she loved to death. Her anxiety grew over the years she loved through death. Her anxiety grew over the years and finally manifested itself in the fear of losing herself, her own death. Every time a friend, acquaintance or family member got seriously ill or died, Joan would panic and feel that *she* would soon become sick and die.

As a vulnerable five-year old, she was too young to understand her loss, and some of its mystery lingered in her mind. Because her mother and brother died of an illness, any illness in her life resurrected those same feelings of fear and dread at losing someone critical to her survival. Finally, after short-term counseling, Joan was able to recognize the anxiety feelings as they arose and to replace them with positive thoughts and feelings. Eventually, she was able to complete the grieving process by acknowledging her love for her mother and letting go of the dependency she still felt as a holdover from her childhood.

At any age, a child is vulnerable when a parent dies. If the parent-child relationship has never progressed to an adult-to-adult relationship, then all of the childhood fears of being abandoned will be reactivated, no matter how old the child is. (The same feelings may be experienced at the death of a stepparent or guardian or grandparent who was a significant figure in one's upbringing.)

Vera was fifty-six when her mother died suddenly of a heart attack. She had always loved and respected her mother as an elder person of authority and power. Even though Vera was a grandmother herself, she acted like a little girl when her mother was around. She would even change her voice and sound like a child when she talked about her mother.

For nearly two years after her mother's death, Vera felt totally abandoned and lost—as a little child might feel. She was devastated by the death. She developed a gastric ulcer, and had one bout after another with the flu. She was virtually unable to conduct her life in a normal way during her grieving period. Finally, after seeking counseling to help her get through these problems, she recognized that she was no longer a child, but an adult. As she accepted this, she became stronger and more self-assured. Her extreme dependency lessened and she was able to release her mother in a healthy way. At a recent wedding in the family, Vera assumed the role of matriarch, replacing her mother in the family hierarchy.

The death of a parent is a particularly profound loss

when a child identifies very strongly with the parent who dies. Often the remaining parent becomes the target of resentment, anger and other strong feelings.

Consider Roger, who felt a strong connection with and respect for his father. When the father died after a long and painful illness, Roger, an engineer who worked in another state, felt guilty about not being around to ease the pain of his father's last year alive.

His father was outgoing, successful in business and had many friends. Roger is just the opposite: quiet, withdrawn and without many friends. In Roger's eyes, his father could do no wrong. Years later, Roger is still carrying around the connection with his father and is stuck in the first stage of grief—denial.

In addition to idealizing his father, Roger always mistrusted his mother. He became convinced that she did not support his dying father the way he would have. He blamed his mother for his father's illness and eventual death. Instead of grieving for his father, Roger generalized his hatred of his mother to all women, a feeling he carried for ten years. He is now forty-three years old, has never married and has had only one relationship with a woman. That woman was thirty-three years his senior, nearly the age of his grandmother . . . the only woman he ever trusted.

Roger will not complete the recovery process and get on with his own life until he accepts the differences between himself and his father. Eventually, Roger must come to terms with remembering his father realistically. He must see that his father was a normal man with faults. Roger must then accept the fact of his father's death.

Psychologically he must bury his father before he can move into the position of the *man* in the family or in any relationship, a role he feels inadequate to fill.

A parent's death can exacerbate other emotional crises going on in a child's life at the same time.

In the movie "Middle Age Crazy," the death of his father is one of the events that triggers the forty-year-old protagonist's fling with irresponsibility. His own aging, his son's departure for college, heavy business responsibilities—and the death of the family patriarch—leave the character pleading, "But I don't want to be the Daddy." So he runs away from his home and has an affair with a cheerleader in an effort to fight off the fast-mounting responsibilities of age.

Because the parent-child roots are so deep, there may be bonds that remain long after the parent has died, as with Roger. Sometimes a child will endeavor to fulfill the uncompleted fantasies or dreams of a parent.

Marge, for example, was the oldest of five children. Her father treated her as the son he wanted for the first six years of her life, until the first son was born. Then gradually as the boy grew big enough to accompany his father on hunting and fishing trips, as Marge had done in the past, her brother replaced her as the close companion of their father.

Marge was twenty-three when her father's sudden death jolted the entire family. Shortly after his death, she applied for admission to law school. She had always planned to become an attorney because that was her father's unfulfilled lifelong dream. She was trying to become something for him that he never became for himself.

She reported great surprise at her feelings of relief and being "off the hook" when she was turned down for admission to law school. When she finally went to graduate school, she followed her own areas of interest, which were not related to law.

At a subconscious level, she had still wanted to please her father and win back the love she felt she was denied after her brother was born. Feeling relieved clued her that she needed to deal further with her father's death, and it helped her get on with her own life.

When the identification with one parent is greater than with the other, the death of that parent naturally has more impact on the child. It also presents a perfect opportunity to confront yourself about buried emotions. If the grieving process is handled completely, in practical and psychological terms, the child can move to new areas of growth and maturity. The death of a parent is a chance to progress, not regress.

Clearing Up Old Business

In western society, where many of our relationships are full of superficial courtesy, there is often a great deal of unfinished "business" when a parent dies. The relationships that are the hardest to clean up and be open and honest about are those charged with emotional content. They are those relationships in which we feel that we have the most to lose if we are honest about our feelings and values and attitudes. Consequently, parents and children may continue to play old roles for years and never treat each other as adults.

I have known people in their forties who are afraid to smoke a cigarette in front of their parents, although they smoke regularly in their daily lives. They argue that they are trying to protect their parents' feelings and respect their position about smoking. Yet their relationship with their parents is dishonest. They are really trying to protect *themselves* from their Mommy's or Daddy's disapproval. They are not secure enough and mature enough to risk disapproval by declaring their independence as adults.

Parents are our first authority figures. When a parent in such a relationship dies, a child may be relieved that she won't have to be phony any longer. But quickly following the relief, she feels guilty for feeling relieved! So she is *not* free. Because the relationship was inauthentic and superficial, the child remained a child, letting her parent's values determine her behavior.

She has to complete her own maturity process of becoming a separate independent adult *after* the parent's death. That may be just as hard to do as when the parent was alive. And if the child can't step out on her own, she may permit the dead parent to continue to have the power of approval and disapproval over her behavior for the rest of her life. The child will carry that mother or father around in her head in the form of messages and consciousness about behaviors. If Mother's still saying that smoking is bad or immoral, then the daughter can't enjoy a cigarette without a twinge of guilt.

Adolescence is the typical time to make a break with parental values, attitudes, and power. But if, as an adult, you still haven't fully made the break, I urge you to do so as soon as possible. It is much more difficult after the parent is dead to break with the parental values and become an independent and self-sufficient person.

Cleaning up relationships with parents can feel extremely frightening and threatening, especially when you know that they disapprove of something that's part of you. One of the best ways is to be sure of what you really have to say or do to feel free and independent. Name-calling and blaming sessions can be avoided if you know what you want to convey to your parents. Spontaneous eruptions of anger and hostility accomplish little and can drive a wedge between you and your parents.

Think through clearly what you want your parents to understand. Then rehearse in your imagination a scene where you tell them. Notice, as you rehearse, any fears, feelings of frustration or anger, or other emotions that you are experiencing, Pay attention to your body also. Be aware of any areas of physical stress, like stomach aches, cramps, headache, changes in breathing, tension along your spine, etc. Most likely you will reexperience old chronic areas of physical tension that you established long ago as a response to childhood fears of the adult authority figure that your parents represented.

As you rehearse and get in touch with emotional and physical tensions and fears, acknowledge them and then let go of them. This may take some effort on your part. Keep going over the same scene until you can do it without any feeling or reaction. It may take several tries, but don't give up. If you get stuck, talk it over with a therapist.

Sometimes, if the issues on which you disagree are too serious, it may be wiser or easier to finish old business using other methods such as writing a letter you never mail, but saying all of the things you wanted to get off your chest and never did. It's best to get professional advice before deciding against a confrontation.

Only after you have completed this rehearsal and planning process should you approach your parents with the issues that you want to clear up. Then make an appointment. Tell them you have something serious that you want to talk to them about, and ask when it's convenient for them to talk to you. If you can predict the amount of time it will take, tell them this too. If *you* set the agenda or the topic of conversation and the length of time you are willing to be with them, then *you* are the one in control of the situation. Most important, you have defused the emotional bomb for yourself. After the first step, things get easier. So you will be able to direct the conversation, and not be subject to getting hooked into old ways of being manipulated.

When you meet with your parents, start by giving them some idea of what you want to talk about. A few introductory words—such as, "This is hard for me to say but I want to do it because it's important to be honest with you"—will give them notice that you intend to assert yourself and are serious about it.

Then be direct and factual with your message. The

simplest way is the best. My friend, the smoker, might say to her parents something like this: "Mother and Dad, I want to tell you that I smoke cigarettes and have for years. I am tired of hiding the fact from you. I intend to continue to smoke at the present time. If you disapprove of my smoking, as I fear you do, I hope that you will not disapprove of *me*. And if you do, then I regret losing your love for now, but I have to be true to myself."

The more serious the matter of disagreement is, the more difficult it will be to discuss with your parents. Telling a staunchly anti-divorce parent that your marriage is over—or a hopeful grandmother that you've decided not to have children—may seem cruel. But it's probably more unkind not to face the issue and to leave your parents wondering or hoping and yourself guilt-ridden. A son who decides not to enter the family business, as his father has always assumed he would do, is dealing with very important values. And one of the hardest moments is to reveal homosexuality to a parent who is horrified by such an idea.

Your parents will naturally follow the long-established patterns of dealing with you—saying no, scolding, threatening punishment. These first reactions could even extend to vowing to cut you out of the will, or threatening to withdraw their love in some way. However, if you are prepared for the worst, then their threats will not work this time. You are standing on your own feet. No matter what the cost, you will have made a major step toward reclaiming your own self.

The most usual parental response is to try the old ways to control you, as when you were their young child. When they realize that it is not working anymore, they will most often relent and accept you as you are. It may take them a little while to come to terms with the changes in your relationship. Give them all the time they need. Remember that you needed time to be able to gain the courage to confront the issue yourself. Offer them time to think about it, and when they are ready and want to discuss the issues further, be available to do so. If your parent is disappointed in you, it's not beyond your control. You've made your step toward redefining the relationship. It's now up to your parents to adjust their expectations.

For your parents, accepting the change may be even harder. They've been used to the old ways perhaps longer than you have. They may greet the news with silence—a form of denial—and may simply decline to talk about it any further. On the other hand, your folks may surprise you and be far more receptive than you expect.

Keep your options open. Few parents are willing to lose contact with their children, and in time they will come around to accepting the changes in you and the changes in your relationship with them. Remember, change is always difficult, particularly where emotions are involved. It requires giving up familiar ways of doing things. Even if the old ways didn't work and weren't honest, they were comfortable, like an old pair of slippers.

Old ways *are* comfortable. You may have a twinge of sadness at throwing away "old friends." But the old ways must go, to make way for new ones. Sometimes the scary part is that you may not know what the new ways of relating to your parents are yet, and since you know the old ways, the old slippers, it may feel safer and less risky to hang on to them.

But it's worthwhile and exciting to move on to new levels of maturity. The second hurdle is still high, but easier than the first.

Once an open dialogue is started with parents, it is easy to keep it that way. The benefits can be enormous. You can begin to relate to each other as real human beings. You learn new things about each other and you may find a depth of love that you never knew was there.

Diane resented her mother for years. Every time Diane would move to a new city, her mother would follow within six months. Her mother was becoming more disabled with respiratory disease and made increasing demands on Diane's time and energy. Prior to the last move, Diane felt angry and resentful. She worked up her courage and told her mother what she was feeling. Both of them were upset for a while. But in the process of talking about the feelings and the alternatives available, both women came to terms with the reality of the situation. Diane and her mother worked out a solution that was comfortable for both.

Her mother moved to the new town, and Diane found her a two-bedroom apartment, then hired a live-in housekeeper to stay in the second bedroom. Diane visited often and took her mother to the doctor and shopping. In the process of working it out, both women were able to deal with the impending death of the mother and be supportive of each other. They became closer than they had ever been, and often both of them were able to express sincere and deep love for each other.

Being able to discuss your parent's health or approaching death is important in being able to finish business between you and say goodbye. But it takes an honesty that must be prepared for by honesty about other matters and feelings.

After a Parent Dies

If your parent is already dead, it is, of course, harder to come to terms with the problem issues in the relationship because a face-to-face encounter is no longer possible. If you find that sorting out the issues is too difficult to do on your own, then see a professional counselor or psychotherapist. Usually short-term counseling can help you become unstuck and let go of the chains of the past.

Unfinished business with their parents is a constant theme I hear from clients. The role of parent, especially of the mother, has been damned and criticized and made very difficult by the changing sex roles and family structure in recent years. If she encouraged self-sufficiency and independence in her children, she may be accused of being cold, distant, or unfeeling. If she was warm and loving, she may be called smothering and manipulative. Parenting is a paradox.

The biggest single way to make progress in grieving for a dead parent or to work out your relationship with a live parent, is to recognize what a difficult job it is to be a parent. Praise them for their victories and forgive them for their trespasses, mistakes, and failures. And take the same attitude for yourself. You were not perfect as a child and, fortunately, you do not have to be perfect now as an adult. Be gentle and loving toward yourself and to those others in your life—living or dead.

Sometimes a son or daughter will carry around a subconscious belief that he or she will die at the same age as, or before, a beloved parent died. Recently a friend lost her husband at forty-eight years old. At the funeral, I expressed condolences and mentioned his age at death. My friend said that she wasn't really surprised by his heart attack and sudden death. Her husband always said that he would die before he was fifty because his father had died at that age, she told me. Clearly this man could not outdo his father by outliving him, and chose to cut short his life when he did.

Another friend, Marlene, whose father died at forty-four, began to get her estate in order about a year before her forty-fourth birthday. She made out a will, appointed an executor of her estate, joined a memorial society, selected the music to be played at her funeral, made arrangements to donate her body organs, and had long discussions with her children about who wanted which keepsakes. She was extremely busy at the time teaching and preparing for an international trip, but she was driven to complete these tasks. As the time got closer to her birthday and to the anniversary of her father's death, she developed severe anxiety and could not explain her pervasive feelings of fear.

Finally, she went to a counselor and realized that she had never completed the grieving process for her father. She had only buried, and repressed, her pain and anger at him for dying and leaving her. Subconsciously she still wanted to be with him, and so she set herself to complete her life at the same time that his life ended. Counseling helped her see what she was doing, and soon she was able to finally bury him, psychologically.

When the grieving process is not effectively dealt with for one parent, the death of the second parent often presents us with an opportunity to complete the process for both parents. When both parents have died, the transition from child to adult, from middle generation to older generation, is completed.

Sometimes there is also a feeling that one life replaces another. In my own family, a niece was born two weeks after the death of her grandfather, and the celebration of welcoming the new child was bittersweet. Yet the grieving was also relieved by joy at the new life.

Another common phenomenon, especially in marriages of many years, is for one spouse to die shortly after the death of a beloved mate, often within a year. The children are faced with the death of both parents in a short period of time. If the couple is very old, the survivor may feel a profound sense of loneliness and have little desire to rebuild a new life. For the widowed one, the wish to join the dead partner becomes so obsessive that he chooses or "wills" himself to die. Such people truly die from a broken heart when death occurs with no apparent physical cause. We know so little scientifically about the will to live and the will to die, yet many of us are familiar with this phenomenon. We all know someone, directly or indirectly, who willed to live, fighting incredible odds to survive, or willed to die, and perished of no discernible cause.

Afterwards

After the funeral, life returns to normal for most people. If, however, you lived in the same house with your parent, then his absence will leave a bigger empty spot and adjustments will have to be made to change daily habits and established routines.

Emotionally, there may be feelings of sadness, anger, depression, and even relief, especially after a long illness that has been painful for the patient and stressful for the family. The emotional responses when a parent dies are generally less acute than with other deaths, and grief is resolved in a shorter period of time, usually six months to a year.

If the parent and children related to each other as independent adults, self-esteem and identity issues are less significant when a parent dies. Frequently adult children have left the nest and made a life of their own, and don't have constant daily contact with their parents.

Soon after the funeral the demands of work and family and other commitments require the bereaved to return to the routines of family life, and the parent's death is pushed or forced into the background.

The death of a parent has the potential for good and bad feelings among sisters and brothers. Property settlement issues can take years to resolve. A clear, explicit will on the part of the parent can help to reduce such difficulties. That is one reason to talk about these things *before* death. Afterwards it is too late.

A parent's death can be the occasion for a renewal of closeness between siblings. Yet sometimes brothers and sisters drift away from each other after their parents die. Political and life-style differences tend to increase the gap. The ongoing love, support, and caring of the large family of aunts, uncles, and cousins is quickly becoming a thing of the past except in a few small communities, and where kinship and religious ties are strong.

Grandchildren

The death of parents may bring you closer to your own children, as you realize that in the normal cycle of life you will someday leave them behind. Grandchildren also grieve for their loss. The severity of grief depends on the closeness of the relationship with the grandparent and the age of the grandchild.

One important aspect is that the death of a grandparent brings the child closer to the reality of the future death of parents. Often a grandparent is the first death loss experience a child has. The way parents handle their own grief becomes a model for children in processing losses through death in the future. If the child had a close intimate relationship with the grandparent, the death may be devastating to the young child.

If the grandchildren are adults when a grandparent dies, they are often the best and closest support their parent has. I asked my grown son how he felt when his grandmother, my mother, died. He said, "I felt a little sad for myself but relieved for you." My mother had been ill for several years before her death. He was able to see the stress her illness produced, primarily for me.

The childless adult often feels truly orphaned if left without any family. He needs to increase friendships and close relationships to assure an ongoing support system.

The death of parents often brings up feelings of our own deaths as we take on the role of family elders. Sometimes there is no one to pass the guard to. It may be sad to imagine leaving no new generation behind, even if one has *chosen* not to have children.

It's important to keep these feelings in perspective during the grieving process. We can't guarantee the future, just as we can't change the past. The succession of generations and the conflicting emotions of grief will soon come into proper focus again, as you return to your normal life.

YOU KNOW YOU'RE MAKING PROGRESS WHEN . . .

...You can remember your child with a smile

...You can realize the painful comments others make are made in ignorance

...You can reach out to help someone else

...You stop dreading holidays

...You can sit through a church service without crying

...You can concentrate on something besides your child

...You can find something to thank God for

...You can be alone in your house without it bothering you

...You no longer feel you have to go to the cemetery every day or every week

...You can tolerate the sound of a baby crying

...You don't have to turn off the radio when his/her favorite music comes on

...You can find something to laugh about

...You can drive by the hospital or that intersection without screaming

...You no longer feel exhausted all the time

...You can appreciate a sunset, the smell of newly mowed grass, the pattern on a butterfly's wings

A Bereaved Parent
Carmel, Indiana

CHAPTER SIX

DEATH OF CHILDREN

The death of a child, especially one's own child, is something the mind can hardly comprehend. It seems to go against nature. The end of a life that is still forming or has just begun is an almost unthinkable cruelty.

But it happens. Parents sometimes must witness the illness or suffering and eventual death of the children to whom they gave birth. And those parents must go on living. They may have other children to care for, they may become parents again later. While nothing will ever fill the empty place that the departed child leaves behind, life goes on for the child's mother and father. Even if your child is gone, you still have a future, as gray and worthless as it may at first seem.

No matter the age of the child, whether baby, young person, adolescent or adult, when children die, the feelings are devastating. The role of parent is to love, protect, teach and nurture your child. Parents *expect* to die before their children. It is the natural order of life events. When the situation is reversed and a child dies before the parents it seems wrong.

Yet we never know why one person dies and another lives. We *do* know that the bereaved survivors must remain and heal and go on with their life. Though death may take your child, the love never goes away.

The grief after a child's death is one of the longest and hardest types of loss to live with. It's necessary to cope with your own emotions and those of other family members. Sometimes when a child has a lingering illness, you also have to cope with his suffering.

Death of a Child Through Illness

Cancer, leukemia, and other forms of malignancy account for most deaths by illness of young children today. When the child and the parents are forewarned of the coming death, there is a chance to work through some of the pain of separation and loss before death occurs.

The question always comes up whether or not to tell a child that he or she is dying. The age of the child is a major consideration in the decision. If she is three years old or more, the truth must be told in a way that she can grasp. Using a story she can understand helps relate directly to her previous experience with death. Perhaps a puppy died, or a goldfish, or a bird, or a distant relative. Referring to that situation will be helpful in explaining the present situation to her. Religious ideas or some concept he or she is curious about can be fit into an explanation of what is happening in your child's life.

The death of a child forces parents to come to terms with their understanding of the *meaning* of death. This is basically what they try to explain to the child—not just the facts of death but some idea of its meaning in religious or spiritual or philosophical terms. That explanation must be given in terms the individual child can understand.

For example, Jim a bright eight-year-old, had a fatal kidney disease. His favorite subject in school was mathematics. He had asked his parents several times about the last number . . . the very *last* number. "I can count to 100, 1,000, 10,000 and more, but what is the last number?" he would ask. His mother told him that numbers didn't end, the last number was called infinity which just went on and on. But Jim didn't understand. When he kept asking about the *last* number, his mother finally said that she didn't know . . . the only one who might know is God. When his parents finally got up the courage to tell Jim about his illness and upcoming death, he said, "Well, now maybe I can find out about the *last* number. When I get to heaven, I will ask God what infinity is."

Jim is typical in his response. Usually the child knows at some level of consciousness that his illness is serious. But the meaning of death to a child will be limited to personal experience and to stories that he may have heard from friends or read in books.

Separation from parents is the closest feeling to death a very young child can relate to. Separation anxiety is a prevailing fear of loss, usually of the mother. Young children will relate to death in these terms, in terms of going away, of leaving, of being alone. They won't feel the sadness or depth of meaning as profoundly as their parents will.

Parents may be worried about breaking down and crying in front of the child. But tears, sadness, and other emotions are natural and real. Putting on a brave, stoic front will not only be phony, but can encourage the child to try to behave the same way and not feel free to cry and express real feelings.

Most reports from dying children (and adults) reveal that what they want and feel comfortable with is reality and truth, sincerity and honesty. Phoniness is confusing and energy-draining. It cheats the dying person of the right to complete the business of life honestly and realistically. Promises of "when you get better," and "when you come home," when everybody *knows* that the child is dying and will never go home, are insults that con you both.

Children are sensitive to non-verbal signals. They know when you are hedging or being dishonest. If your words do not match your facial expression or what your body reveals, it is confusing to your child. He will know when you are lying. Children take the clues for their behavior from your behavior. Be open and responsive with your words and your actions. Feel free to express love, sadness and any other emotions as they arise, so your child can feel free to express his feelings too.

Answer all of the child's questions as openly and honestly as you can. If you don't know the answer, find out. Your doctor and hospital staff are employed by you; you are paying for their services. You do not need their approval of what *you tell your child*. Be assertive in requesting that they be honest with your child and about any special services or considerations you may want or need.

After you have told your child the truth in language he or she can understand, it is important to let the child's own natural grieving process take over. Age, personality, and patterns of handling stress and change will dictate how your child will work it out. Remember: the child's way will probably not be your way, so let the child do it *his or her* way. A quiet, shy child may not want to talk about it or want any of her friends to know. An outgoing boy may want to continue to play Little League baseball as long as possible. A teen-ager may want to live long enough to go to the prom. From grade school on, friends' attitudes become increasingly important. Help your child to continue to live as normally as possible. Keeping relationships with friends and school-mates will make the final months and days easier.

Sometimes when radical drug therapy (chemo-therapy) is used, there are side effects, such as causing the patient's hair to fall out. This can be very difficult for a child to accept. Surgery, scars, tumors, open wounds, and other disfiguring physical changes will require special caring and love and support from family and friends.

Each time something that results in physical change happens, the child will have a separate grieving process. He will experience little pieces of his death. And each little piece will be mourned. Feelings of denial, anger, frustration, depression, and worry about what his friends will think or say will all come up for him before he will be ready to accept the change. Tell the child you understand these feelings and you love him. Don't try to deny or downplay his distress or he'll have conflicting feelings.

Sometimes parents or neighbors can learn to give injections and other medical treatments that permit the child to stay at home. If your child can spend the last months or weeks at home, try to treat the child the way you always have. Let sisters and brothers spend time with the sick one. Let them squabble and play as usual. The more normal the situation, the better.

If you have been a physically demonstrative family, then continue to touch the dying child as much as or more than before. Touch is a wonderful way to communicate, to show your love and acceptance. Patting, rocking, stroking, washing and combing hair, and grooming are all good ways to say, "I love you," without words. This is a way for brothers and sisters to be close.

Death of a Child by Accident

"I always felt that the worst thing that could happen to me was for one of my children to die, to be killed. I used to think that I would die too, that if someone came to my door or called me on the telephone and said that one of my children was dead, that I would die on the spot. I always wanted to die before any of my children did. I wanted the deaths in our family to be in the right order, first parents at old age, then the children.

"When my daughter died, I wanted to die for a long time. Sometimes I still do, and that was almost two years ago. When I heard the news of her death, I was immediately in shock. I was numb, floating like in a dream, a nightmare really, that I couldn't wake up from. I seemed to stay that way for a long time . . . for months. Then gradually I came out of it, and now I am still alive and Cindy is dead."

Mary Kay, a member of a support group of people who have lost children through death, told her story the first night the group met. Her seventeen-year-old daughter, an honor student, had gone to a party with some friends on the night of their high school graduation. On the way home their car hit another car head-on. Three of the students were killed, including Cindy, and three more seriously injured.

In some fatal injuries, there is a little time before the death takes place. This warning time may ease the shock a bit. One family had a few days to adjust to losing a two-year-old son who had accidentally inhaled fumes from paint thinner. He lingered for a few days in a hospital as his lung tissues deteriorated. Then he died quietly in his sleep. The parents were numb with disbelief and shock. The child's father, who was with him at the time of the accident, experienced a great deal of guilt.

Those few days that the parents had to get used to the idea of the accident and the possibility of the death gave them a brief head start in their mourning process. As a general rule, the more forewarning you have, the faster the recovery from grief will be, although reactions, of course, vary from person to person.

Accidents by their very nature imply a wrongdoing. When a child dies accidentally, the survivors often feel terrible guilt and blame.

Tony, a four-year-old boy who ran into the street to buy an ice cream from a vendor, was hit by a car. As he lay dying in the hospital, he kept saying over and over, "I'm sorry, Mommy, don't be mad at me." He had been told a hundred times not to run into the street and warned of the dangers of automobiles, but his impulse for ice cream was greater than his concern for safety.

Tony felt guilty and feared rejection from his parents because he got caught disobeying them. His mother felt guilty because she had given him money to buy the ice cream on his own. He had on other occasions success-fully bought ice cream on his own, under his mother's supervision. Subconsciously she was furious with him for disobeying her, for doing this to her, for getting hurt and for dying. Her mixed emotions added to her an-guish.

The tragedy of a child's accidental death is that it seems so unnecessary and unfair. The child's life has been snuffed out so early, so prematurely. The parents and the driver of the car take a mental snapshot or have a movie in their minds of the incident. They play the film over and over again. Wondering, speculating, wishing, planning, thinking, trying to understand, to rearrange, to change the accident. Trying to live with the loss. Trying to go on and live. Trying to remember and trying to forget all at the same time. Wishing they could mentally will time to move backward, somehow erase what happened. Wishing it had been you instead of your child. And feeling guilty for being alive. And feeling sorry for yourself that you are. Feeling sorry that you cannot escape the sadness and the loss and the confusion and pain.

When an adult dies, and his parents survive, the emotions may be just as intense as if they had lost their son or daughter in childhood. The older person won-ders, "Why her, when she had so many years ahead? Why not me? I'm old; I've lived." The parents may sincerely wish they could trade places with the dead child.

The Family

Saying goodbye to your child will be one of the hardest tasks you'll ever do. Everyone in the family will be affected by this death. It will seem unbearably painful—but it can also be an opportunity to learn a lot about yourself. Sharing this common experience can be a chance to grow and to become closer to other members of your family. Sometimes life's most painful tasks can be lessons that move us to another place in our development as individuals and as a family.

After the death and the funeral are over, you will need some time to adjust and rest. If you have worked through some of your feelings during the illness, it will be a little easier and somewhat faster for you to recover and to get through your mourning. You will need at least a month or two to break the everyday habits of having that child around. There will be little reminders to keep you remembering, such as toys, clothes, or other personal belongings.

Holidays, photographs, the bedroom, friends from the neighborhood or school will all hit you with renewed sadness as you realize that your child is gone. Accept these things and let your feelings surface as they are ready. As soon as possible, get rid of as many reminders around the house as you can. Give away the clothes and toys and personal belongings. Put away the photographs for a while. Paint and redecorate the bedroom, get new furniture if possible. You may save one or two things as keepsakes, but put them away for now.

Gradually, as you do these things, you will find yourself letting go of your child as you clear out the old and make room in your life for someone or something new. You will begin to build the next part of your life. Don't force yourself to do these things, but don't delay either. Do them as you feel ready to. Each step will lead you closer to acceptance of the death. You are not denying that your child lived—you are helping yourself heal and go on with life.

Slowly, in time, you will notice that you are dwelling on the child less and less. And when you do, the feelings will be less painful. You will start to look forward to things again. When you do think or talk about your dead child, you'll remember both good and the not-so-good things about her or him. No one is perfect, and it is important to remember your child in a realistic way, and in happier, healthier times as a normal youngster.

The time of recovery will vary from person to person. We are all unique and we grieve in different ways. If you have allowed yourself to cry and to feel your sadness and anger and other feelings, you should begin to accept the reality of the death in sometime after six months. If you get stuck, get some counseling. Talk to friends or join a group of parents going through a similar experience. Compassionate Friends is a good self-help group. There is a lot of comfort in knowing that you are not alone in your grief and pain. You may be able to give some comfort to other people . . . helping others is a good way to help yourself.

The role of religion can be important in your grieving process. If you have faith in God or some other power *higher than here on earth*, or if you believe in reincarnation, you may take a type of comfort in your mourning process from believing death is not the final end. Religious belief is, of course, an individual matter. For some parents, the tragedy of losing a child has shaken their ability to believe in a just God or a meaning in life. Some people may in time return to their faith. Even if your fundamental beliefs are shaken, you must work through your bitterness and anger.

The first few months after the child's death will be filled with regrets, wishes and feelings all confused and mixed together, all painful and overwhelming and seeming unbearable. As the parent, you are torn apart inside. Your mixed and powerful feelings are normal—because you are experiencing one of the most dreaded events that can occur in life. But—as impossible as it may seem—you are still alive and you will go on living.

Norma told a group of other bereaved parents who had lost a child, "I was floating in a black void when my daughter was dying. Nothing was real—it was a continual nightmare every day and every night." Other parents understood her experience.

Martha shared her behavior at the funeral. "At my son's funeral I consoled everyone else. I told them all 'It's going to be okay.' I had a need to talk incessantly to anyone who would listen. I drove people away from me. I wore them out." Many parents need the same loving, listening support. We need time to get it out—to talk, cry, rage and laugh during this time of pain and anguish.

It helps to keep the old patterns of your life going as much as possible. If you have a job, keep working, even part-time. Stay as involved as possible in outside activities. Make a list of people who will listen. Talk with friends and family members about your feelings when you need to. Seeing a professional counselor may be very helpful. Let go of grudges and guilt, and don't blame yourself and others. Nothing is to be gained by holding onto resentment, hate, anger, or hostility. They won't bring your child back or ease your sense of loss. Such feelings can become barriers between you and others and can cause serious illness in the long run. This is especially important for wives and husbands.

More than ever before, this is the time when family

members should be supportive and caring and loving toward each other. Everyone is experiencing a private hell. A death in the family affects all of the members, individually and together.

Support, care, and love are nurturing activities. They are something that we usually think of "giving" to someone else but sometimes we need to make sure we receive this nurturing. In our society, women have been the main nurturers. But when a mother is in deep grief and mourning, she is thrown back on whatever reserve resources she may have to nurture herself to survive, with little or nothing left over to give others. In fact, now is the time that she needs help *from* others.

The father may be in a dreadful state of grief, but not able to express his pain in a direct way. He may start drinking heavily, staying away from home, or withdraw into a depression. He may suffer needlessly by resisting the simple but important act of crying. Until recently, men have been neither encouraged nor rewarded for nurturing or for expressing their feelings of doubt and helplessness. It is hard for many men to give their wives the kind of support they need. When a man is nurturing, it is usually a one-shot attempt, and if they feel awkward or clumsy, they give up and don't try again.

If a man is trying to be strong to comfort his wife, he may block his own emotions. Yet he often struggles with feelings about failing in his role as protector of the family or problem solver who "fixes" things. If he has been brought up to feel self-sufficient, he will have trouble admitting that he needs help.

A woman may misunderstand her husband's stoic ways, his refusal to talk about the child, his eagerness to return to work and normalcy. She is more likely to express her grief through crying and talking, and she thinks that if he isn't doing the same that he's not feeling pain.

Both need to understand and be patient with each

other and encourage each other to get their feelings out.

What both parents need is not one attempt, but a sustained effort at just being available for each other. Listen without judging. Touching, hugging, and showing signs of kindness are easy ways to be supportive and nurturing, and they can be so meaningful. Don't worry about trying to say or do the "right thing." Just be there, cry and hold each other.

Ted, sixteen, broke his neck in a high school football game and died immediately. He was the youngest child in the family. His mother went into shock and depression and refused to talk to anyone. She wouldn't leave her home. She sat for hours at a time and just stared at the walls. Ted's father began to drink heavily to try to blot out his pain, both for the loss of his son and the frustration and confusion he felt over his wife's behavior. The mother blamed her husband for the accident because he had encouraged, even pushed, the boy to play football. Within eight months after the death of the son, the couple got a divorce, a double loss for both of them. Instead of being supportive to each other in their loss, they lost each other.

The number of couples who divorce after a child dies is shockingly high—some say up to eighty percent of marriages end within two years after a child dies. I believe with professional help—individual, marriage and bereavement counseling—many of these divorces could be avoided.

Families as a unit have coping styles, and each individual member of a family has a unique method of coping. When any change effects the family, these coping mechanisms come into play. Coping styles are patterns of behavior that are triggered internally and acted out externally.

Seeds of how the family system handles crisis are already established in most families before a major life event like a death happens. Some families pull closer together, some divide and go their separate ways temporarily. In other families, one individual may undermine the other members' sense of reality and deny any experience of an event that is different from his own.

For example, a father may blame the driver of an automobile in which his daughter is killed for drinking and driving. He may develop an abnormal hatred of that person and displace his grief at the loss of his child. When others in the family encourage him to allow his feelings of sadness and loss to surface he may become very angry and say something like, "If John hadn't been drinking, Jennie would be alive now. It's all his fault." His wife may say tearfully, "I miss Jennie so much; she is constantly on my mind." In this case neither person is responding to the grieving process of the other. This is crazy-making behavior and can be very divisive and destructive.

In Jennie's family, the death of their daughter was the final crisis event that brought to a head negative patterns of interacting that had gone on for years. If family members recognize that each is trying to cope with grief, they can be more helpful and comforting to each other.

For single parents, support can be found from friends and relatives. Don't hesitate to ask those close to you to listen to your feelings.

Grandparents will feel a tremendous surge of pain at two levels—for the loss of the child and at seeing their own children so badly hurt and being unable to help. Permitting grandparents a role in helping with ordinary errands and household chores will help in their healing.

Other Children Suffer Too

Don't forget the needs of the surviving children in the family. They will suffer from the death of a brother or sister. Subconsciously, they may feel responsible. They will have fears about their own death.

Reactions vary, of course, from child to child, but will follow each child's predictable pattern of adjusting to stress and change. Some children will have sleeping problems, such as waking at unusual hours and having nightmares. Some may begin wetting the bed, or resume thumb-sucking. Others may begin to act out in ways that get attention, if not the reassurances of love from their parents, by misbehaving at school or home.

Paul and Jeff, twelve- and thirteen-year-old brothers, were playing near a river when Jeff slipped and fell into the ice-cold water and drowned. Paul had been an excellent student and an outstanding baseball player before the accident. Jeff, a year older, was the spontaneous, risk-taking one. After the accident, Paul became restless, did poorly in school, wore dirty clothes, quit baseball and generally lost interest in life. He would go and sit by Jeff's grave for hours. The parents were in such distress themselves for about six months that they didn't realize how much trouble Paul was having. Finally, they tried counseling through the school, and that helped some. Eventually, the family moved to another town. The new location didn't have all of the old reminders of Jeff, and soon Paul began to do well in school again. Eventually, he was able to let go of the terrible guilt he carried about not being able to prevent his brother's death.

Children are easily overlooked when a family is in mourning. But they must also mourn in order to continue to live their own lives in a healthy way. They need added support, love, reassurance, and a chance to talk about their feelings, including negative ones, toward the dead sibling. Children who don't express these thoughts may carry unresolved death anxieties into adult life. If fears get shoved inside and buried in the subconscious, they will emerge and haunt the child in later life.

Small children may have overwhelming curiosity

about the details of the burial, such as wondering why Jody is being put in the ground if heaven is in the sky. These questions are the child's way of learning to his own satisfaction what this business of dying means.

A child may feel guilty for fighting with his sister, may wonder if he is going to die soon too, may be preoccupied with his sibling's toys or clothing. All of these are thoughts appropriate to his age and ability to understand, and adults must reassure their children in whatever way he asks.

CHAPTER SEVEN

DEATH BEFORE OR AFTER BIRTH

A child lost through miscarriage or stillbirth or in other ways at the beginning of life is not as fully formed in personality as a child several months or years old. Yet there is still grief involved, sometimes worsened by hopes and expectations for the new baby.

When a physically defective or mentally retarded child is born, there is a sense of loss and pain in realizing that the child will never live a full life. Parents must contemplate the extra demands that care of such a child will mean. Some are able to accept the responsibility with love; others realize they don't have the emotional resources for such a life. The conflicts of grieving may continue for years, unless parents work through their emotions to a resolution.

Miscarriages

In medical language, all miscarriages are called abortions, whether the pregnancy is terminated deliberately or by a natural process. To abort means to shorten, to remain undeveloped. The primary difference between a miscarriage and what we call an abortion is that the miscarriage is not desired by the pregnant woman, and is generally caused by some physical problem. An abortion, on the other hand, is the surgical or chemical intervention to interrupt and end the pregnancy, and is usually desired by the woman, who often did not intend to get pregnant. Both cases involve psychological pain, distress and grief.

After five years of trying every drug and technique, Sally was delighted when she finally became pregnant. The pregnancy was fine until the fourth month, when she started spotting and having cramps. A few weeks later, the doctor told her that the baby was dead inside her and that she would probably begin to abort the fetus soon. At first Sally refused to believe the doctor. She had already bought diapers and baby clothes. Slowly, as time went on and she realized that she did not feel the baby move in her womb, she accepted the fact of the death.

Finally, after two months of waiting and no sign of natural abortion, the doctor decided to do a surgical abortion. Sally almost died during this simple procedure. She hemorrhaged and had to be given several pints of blood. In a few days she went home full of someone else's blood and no baby. Sally's grief was tremendous because she thought that this would be her only chance to have a baby. She held onto it physically and emotionally as long as possible. Eventually she worked through her feelings, and a year or so later she was pregnant again.

While Sally's situation is more complex than many miscarriages, the loss of an expected child can be cruelly disappointing for both parents. It may be especially hard for the woman because it is her body and she must make the physical adjustment from pregnancy to non-pregnancy and non-motherhood. Psychologically she may feel like a failure.

In some cases there may be feelings of relief, especially if the pregnancy was untimely. But, having adjusted to expecting a baby and anticipating the birth, it's a shock and loss when suddenly there is no baby. It may not be a long-term adjustment, but it is painful for a while.

One woman told me that the worst part was explaining to well-meaning people who kept asking her if she still had morning sickness. It was difficult for her to go through the whole story again and again. She resented the invasion of her privacy. The best way to handle such questions is to tell people simply and honestly that you have had a miscarriage. And if they pry, say that you don't want to discuss the details because it is painful for you.

Stillbirth and SIDS

Women who deliver a baby that is dead or dies immediately may be plagued with questions about burial, naming the child and what to tell friends. They may feel guilt, as if they did something wrong that caused the death.

Especially when the birth was carefully planned, the absence of a baby is devastating.

There are many symptoms and emotions of grieving. Parents report that they often wonder months or years later if the experience was real. Friends may seem to think the episode should be forgotten quickly.

Parents need to work through their grief patiently before making decisions about another pregnancy.

The Sudden Infant Death Syndrome, or crib death, is particularly baffling. An apparently healthy baby is found dead in its bed.

SIDS is the major cause of death in infants after the first week of life, and it affects about two of every 1,000 live births. Physicians don't fully understand the causes or have any means of preventing or predicting its occurrence.

Parents inevitably feel responsible for a SIDS death, although there is no reason to take such blame—SIDS is probably caused by subtle defects that doctors don't know how to identify.

The National Sudden Infant Death Syndrome Foundation in Landover, Maryland, has information that may help families grieving for this type of death. (See Appendix B.)

Abortion

Abortion, of course, differs from a miscarriage in that it requires a conscious decision on the part of the woman to terminate a pregnancy. Few women take such a decision lightly. I have seen many women struggle with the conflict of an unwanted pregnancy and the decision of whether to end a potential life. Even if she decides an abortion is best, she may still grieve as for a dying child. Much of the grieving is done before the abortion, during the decision-making process. Afterwards, for a few days, weeks, or months, it is not unusual for the woman to experience some sadness when thinking about the abortion. Again, she must work through all her feelings or the loss may haunt her forever.

The hardest part is making the decision to have an abortion in the first place. Generally, such a decision is tied to conflict. If you are pressured to get the abortion against your wishes through threats by the father ("If you have the kid I will have nothing to do with you"), bribery ("I'll pay for it, dear"), or through shame ("What will the neighbors say?"), you may have a much more difficult time in processing the grief later. The final choice must be made by the woman herself. No amount of coercion for or against the abortion by parents, lover, husband or friends will lead to the "right" decision for you.

All of the stages of grief will be there. A woman who learns she is unintentionally pregnant will first react with denial and disbelief. The first part of the grief cycle is a wish that "it isn't true," "not now," "not me." Her second reaction will probably be anger—at the father for not accepting some responsibility for birth control or for being sexually demanding at the wrong time. You may also be angry at yourself for the same reasons. The constant worry about an unwanted pregnancy will overshadow everything in your life at this time.

The next stage will be bargaining. You may wish for some "natural" event to occur that will end the pregnancy so you won't have to decide. Or you may try to make a "deal" with God to never do anything wrong for the rest of your life if only He will make the pregnancy go away or give you a "sign" that you should have the baby, or in some way help you to get out of this mess.

The fourth stage is depression or feeling low or down. At this stage you experience all your unresolved emotions including guilt, anger, disappointment, and sadness. You have to face key conflicts. You may feel that by having an abortion you are giving up a part of yourself and a child of yours. You must deal with concerns such as abandoning a potential life, or the moral issue of killing a being with a soul. During this stage there may be a lot of tears and feelings of self-pity. It's better to feel those things than to try to be stoic and keep very strong emotions inside. Take as long as you need to work through this part of the process. Stay with your sadness and your pain. In a short time you will know what the right decision is for you.

Acceptance is the final stage of grieving. If you have decided to go ahead and get the abortion, you will now be able to make the necessary arrangements and follow them through. In the early stages of the pregnancy, an abortion can usually be handled by a safe and simple procedure in a doctor's office. There is little or no physical pain. There may still be psychological pain or regrets, but if you worked through the grieving process, you will be able to reduce the time of inner conflict and get on with your life.

A woman who decides to complete an unplanned pregnancy will be sure she has made the right decision if she knows she has weighed her choices.

Adoption

Putting an infant or child up for adoption is a difficult choice that some women face. And it is a loss that creates grief.

Consider Maggie. She found herself pregnant with her lover's child. She was thirty-eight at the time, divorced with two teen-age daughters. She didn't want to have an abortion, but she also didn't want to raise another child. So she talked the situation over with her lover. He agreed to support her during the pregnancy and to pay for the delivery of the baby, provided that she put the infant up for adoption.

She agreed, and she saw the baby only in the viewing room. Maggie released him with love to begin life with his new parents. Now she sometimes misses him because she had always wanted a son. She thinks of him sometimes and wonders what he looks like and how he is doing in school. But she has few regrets about her decision.

Maggie was mature enough to make a rational decision. But many women in similar circumstances are not. Becoming pregnant is a major event in a woman's life, and giving up a child is like letting go of an important part of her. With a growing number of teen-age pregnancies, the problem is a frequent one and difficult for the individuals involved. It is an increasing dilemma for society.

Along with sexual activity must go the ability to respond to the risk of pregnancy. That's what responsibility is—the ability to respond. The responsibility for pregnancy belongs to both partners in any sexual relationship.

Traditionally, women have been the ones to pay the price of an unplanned pregnancy. But it takes two people, male and female, to create a child or a pregnancy, and both of these people should share equal responsibility for either the prevention of the pregnancy or for the creation of new life. One of the things a man can do is ask a woman if she might become pregnant if they have sex. If she's not using any birth control measures, then they should refrain, or he should use a contraceptive.

Still, there are times when precautions fail and pregnancy occurs. Mark learned after his high school graduation that Sue, whom he had slept with once, was pregnant. Mark had asked Sue if she was using a method of birth control, and she said she was on the "pill." She *was* on the "pill," but had taken it only for a few days and it was not yet effective.

Both young people agonized over their dilemma. They did not really love each other. Mark planned to go to college and could not afford to support a wife and child. They talked over the options, including abortion, with her parents and his mother. Finally, Sue decided to have the child on her own. Her parents stood by her, and Mark checked with her often, even though he lived in another city. She worked and earned enough money to pay for her pre-natal care and delivery. A few years after her son was born, she fell in love and married and her husband adopted her little boy.

Only a few years ago this story would have had another ending. The couple would have been forced to marry, and another marriage would have been based on a short-term spontaneous sexual encounter, and would most likely have developed into a relationship built on resentment and anger rather than on mutual love and respect.

In the process of deciding what to do about the pregnancy, all parties were able to think about future consequences, of various courses of action and to come to terms with their feelings of grief and loss created by the situation. Sue chose to not let Mark see the baby after he was born. Recently, Mark told me that every time he sees a cute, blond three-year-old, he feels a sense of longing and regret at not being able to see and be involved with his son. His mother says that she, too, feels sad that is not able to be a grandparent to the child.

Though the aftermath was difficult for all parties, the decision had to be the mother's. Others must take comfort in knowing that the best thing was done for the mother and child. People closely involved in an un-planned pregnancy feel many of the emotions of grief when they lose contact with the child. They must—as with a death—let themselves feel the pain, then let it go, and move on into the future.

Many situations in life involve loss and are difficult and painful, but they can also be wonderful opportuni-ties to grow and to develop sensitivity about our future encounters and to have more empathy for others. We do not always get what we think we want in life, and maybe it is a blessing in disguise.

CHAPTER EIGHT

DEATH OF FRIENDS AND SIBLINGS

Death of Friends

When a close friend dies, especially if the person is about the same age and the same sex as you, it often forces you to consider your own death. The effect can be startling. The death of a friend is often a milestone event—an occurrence that leads to rethinking and possibly rearranging personal priorities. Because we may identify so strongly with a close friend, that person's death brings up reminders of our mortality more than the death of a parent, child or spouse may do.

The more you have in common with the friend, the more his death will make you contemplate and wonder about your own. Sometimes a surviving friend will realize, "It could just as easily have been me." Such a death has a way of reminding us how vulnerable we are, how fragile life sometimes is. And it may cause you to reassess the direction of your own life.

Jack's story is a good example. A successful stock market broker making a lot of money, Jack didn't spend as much time with his family as he wanted. His job was demanding and required him to work long hours. But about three years ago one of his best friends, a man who worked in the same office, had a heart attack. He died while celebrating his twin daughters' eighteenth birthday in a restaurant. The man was fifty-one years old. Jack was thirty-nine at the time.

Not long after his friend's death, Jack started to have chest pains during stressful business meetings. Finally, he had a good physical check-up including an electrocardiogram. He received a clean bill of health. But the chest pains continued. He kept thinking of the death of his friend. Jack thought about how much his friend missed in life by not watching his children develop as adults. He saw how tough it was for his friend's widow to manage for the first year or so.

Jack realized that these concerns were projections of worries about his own death. He didn't want his life to end that way. He talked his feelings over with his wife and children and decided to quit his job and change his life-style. The family moved to a smaller town, bought an older house and remodeled it as a family project. Jack is now the proprietor of a small art gallery. He is relaxed, has gotten reacquainted with his children, and says that he has never been so happy in his life. And he has had no more chest pains.

The impact of a death of someone outside the immediate family will depend on several factors, including the length of the relationship, the intensity of the relationship, the circumstances of the death, the age of the survivor, the survivor's prior experiences with death, and the emotional connection between the two.

When I was in the fourth grade, we lived in a small farming community in Michigan. The few Mexican families who lived in a small barrio there were laborers who picked sugar beets. One child from the barrio, Maria, and I would stay on the playground long after school was over and she would teach me Spanish. She was polite and bright and shy. Our friendship flourished and in a few months we became best friends.

I remember the shock and sadness I felt the day I went to school and was told that Maria had been hit by a car the afternoon before, sometime around five o'clock, as she walked home after our Spanish lesson. Our class visited the funeral home. I felt a profound sense of loss. Afterwards I remembered the words that she taught me. I paid a lot more attention to cars when I crossed the street after that. And I have always had a special place in my heart for Mexicans.

Though most people understand that someone who loses a family member grieves, fewer people realize the special circumstances and trauma that one goes through when an intimate friend becomes ill or has a fatal disease or accident.

Death of Lovers

When someone's lover dies, there is not always a place for the aggrieved survivor to turn for comfort—especially if the lover is married or the two were of the same sex. Neither extramarital affairs nor homosexual relationships are usually sanctioned by society, and many people—sometimes even close friends and relatives—fail to realize the sympathy that the survivor of such a loss needs.

Marriage is still the predominantly accepted bond between adults. And most other relationships are formed within social institutions such as the family, school, church, neighborhood or workplace. People who live outside the prevailing social norms are frequently penalized by discrimination, non-acceptance, fear, rejection and hostility. Often the relationship is kept secret, and many acquaintances may not realize what a loss someone has suffered if they're not aware of the person's intimate connection with a recent death.

It is difficult to assess the number of people who are affected by such situations. But I would guess that the number is much higher than most people imagine—possibly twenty percent of the population fit into one category or the other at sometime in their lives. Because of the negative attitudes that prevail in society, most people are reluctant to take the risk of openly revealing such intimate relationships. Since discretion is the predominant behavior pattern in such a relationship, the person involved is often without a support system when a deep loss occurs.

A former student came to class extremely distraught one night. Let's call her Lynn. Her married lover in a seven-year relationship had just had a stroke and was in the hospital. He couldn't talk and was very ill. Lynn got the news from neighbors in his apartment building. When she called the hospital to see how he was, she had to lie about her relationship to him, saying that she was his sister. She got sketchy news of his condition and found out that his wife and daughter were keeping a constant vigil. Lynn wanted to go to him, and she knew that he would want her there. Yet if she went and created a scene, it would be worse for everyone. Lynn was so worried about her lover and was so full of conflict about her options. She felt shut out of his life.

He recovered for a short time and went home to live with his wife for three months before his second and final stroke. During that time, Lynn's life was a nightmare. She was beside herself with yearning to be with him and fears about his health. She never had a chance to talk to him again. She saw the notice of his death in the obituary column of the newspaper. When Lynn went to the funeral, she sat in the back row, a widow without support, suffering her loss in solitude, crying her tears alone.

Lesbians and gay men suffer the same lack of support from society at large. In the past decade, gays have received more understanding and acceptance through some political and educational activism and media ex-

posure. Yet our society still discriminates against homo-
sexuals.

This results in little or no support from the usual
places—family, friends, and fellow workers—when one
partner dies, particularly if the relationship is still "in
the closet."

Many gay people, especially older ones, have not
revealed their sexual preference to relatives, neighbors,
fellow workers, and others. Most gay couples, however,
have a circle of trusted friends and these friends become
the caring support system. People are people, and when
someone you love dies or is injured or stricken by a fatal
disease, the anxiety and fear of losing the lover is very
painful emotionally. It is helpful to have acknowledgment and support from the people in your social environment, but grieving is a solitary experience, and you
will do your own grieving in your personal, unique way,
with or without the support of others.

Death of Siblings

The death of a brother or sister is usually a major loss,
although several factors need to be considered. The ages
of the siblings, the closeness of the relationship and the
resolution of sibling rivalry are some important considerations.

Brothers and sisters have the potential for the longest
relationships in the life span. When young children
suffer the loss of a sister or brother, it is often a
confusing mystery. Sometimes they feel guilty that they
caused the death because they wished for the death or
for the other to "go away forever" in a moment of anger.
Or they may feel that they could have done something
heroic to save the life of the other—or in case of an
accident that they should have died instead of the one
who did.

It's important to explore these feelings with children

and allow them to express both negative and positive feelings toward their deceased brother or sister.

When adult siblings die, the emotional impact is usually reduced. Often their lives have taken them in different directions and the intensity of early childhood connections begins to fade. There is often a profound feeling of sadness and sorrow, like losing some part of yourself. It is losing a part of your past, of common experiences and parents and places. Brother and sister relationships are the longest ongoing relationships in our lives.

There is, of course, a difference if you are close by during a long period of illness and gradual deterioration. You will feel the impact of the death more than if you have had a long separation by years and/or distance. Adult siblings often find they are very different from each other in interests, values and personalities. If there are conflicts between you that were not cleared up before the death, you may experience guilt or regret or other unresolved feelings. But the connecting bonds of their parents and childhood experiences remain. In other cases, brothers and sisters will again live together or close to each other after their families have been raised. The main effect of a sibling death is to remind you of your own vulnerability or aging and what a fragile gift your own life is.

Death of Others

We also grieve over the deaths of people who are not part of our immediate family, friends, or lovers. A former teacher, minister, or mentor may die, and even if you have not been in contact with them for years, you may feel deep sadness and loss.

There are times when an entire country will be in mourning when the head of state, while holding office, is assassinated. For example, the world reeled when

President John Kennedy was killed. The shock and horror of his assassination threw this country into mass mourning. Almost every American old enough to remember 1963 can recall what he or she was doing on that fateful day.

The murder of musician John Lennon in December 1980 also touched off a worldwide outpouring of grief. As the most creative member of the Beatles, a revolutionary group in music, he had expressed the feelings of millions of young people for twenty years. People all over the world strongly identified with him, and when he was assassinated during a time of renewed personal creativity in his life, thousands of young people and adults felt the loss very deeply.

To some people, the death of an admired mentor or culturally important person may be more affecting than any loss they have experienced of members of their own families. Many times the deaths of key entertainment figures are followed by several suicides among fans. There is a fascination with the deaths of folk heroes such as James Dean, Rudolph Valentino, Marilyn Monroe or Elvis Presley.

Collective grief is experienced on different levels. First are the subjective or personal feelings of loss which vary according to how strongly you felt about the person who has just died. Secondly, you come face-to-face with your own vulnerability and the fact that life can be snuffed out so quickly. A third issue to confront is the potential violence that lies so close to the surface in "civilized" human beings. The political or cultural aftermath can have an impact for years.

Seeing violence across the world daily in the news or in fictionalized television shows does not really have the impact that the death of a "real" person has, even if we do not know that individual personally.

Grief is experienced collectively when several people share similar feelings at the same time. Anxiety and fears for an orderly transition from the initial chaos of an assassination to new leadership prevail among those affected. They may share feelings of anger and outrage and want to get even with the killer. Because this is not possible for them as individuals, their frustrations may make them feel impotent, powerless, out of control, and paranoid, as if victimized by a psychotic or an international plot.

Rumors and paranoid fears run rampant. Such a death becomes a "media event," and it is almost impossible to carry on life in a regular way. The rituals of a state funeral or an observation of mourning are necessary to allow some time for a cooling off from negative feelings. The rituals of the funeral are for the living.

Assassination attempts have a similar effect, but do not carry the same degree of impact as a death. In a shorter period, the country returns to normal and individuals resume their usual activities. But lingering fear or sadness remains for some time after the event.

The deaths of Robert Kennedy, Mahatma Gandhi, and Martin Luther King dramatize the emotional power of a public figure cut down in his prime. Through the senselessness of their untimely deaths, they may in fact have had more impact on social change than they had through their living words and actions.

Unlike life, death cannot be taken away
from man, and therefore we may consider it is the gift of God.

—Seneca

CHAPTER NINE

DEATH OF SELF:
THE DYING PROCESS

One of the most challenging experiences of the human condition is to come to terms with being alone. We spend most of our lives being involved in one relationship after another. Most people go from living with parents to living with a spouse or lover, then to becoming parents themselves. Even those without families are usually wrapped up in friendships, work relationships, social activities or projects and other ways of connecting with people. We continually seek and desire being around others. As a result, we think we need others to complete us and make us whole.

People often stay in destructive and unhappy relationships because at some deep level they fear being lonely or being left alone. When we relate to others, we have the illusion of being secure; we want to be taken care of and loved. We fear loneliness because we're afraid that we can't take care of ourselves and meet our own needs. Everyone experiences this anxiety of being alone to some extent.

The fear of being alone began when we were infants, when we were truly helpless and dependent on another for our very survival. So great is our need for another human being during infancy that subconsciously we continue to seek security in our relationships with other human beings as adults. And we fear losing them. We think that only through others can we avoid discomfort and relieve our fears. In extreme cases of insecurity a person may feel worthless and think that life has no meaning and no fulfillment unless it is shared with someone else.

Loneliness is associated with feelings of separation, isolation, losing contact and abandonment. For some, the thought of being alone conjures up feelings of anguish, despair, desolation, panic and terror—the worst possible fate.

The reality of the human condition is that we are always, essentially alone. The *challenge* of the human condition is to come to terms with our singularity, our uniqueness. No one else can live your life. You are born alone and you die alone. No one else experiences the events in life in exactly the same way you do, not a spouse or a child or a close sibling or a best friend. Your thoughts, impressions, values and decisions are yours alone. When you are dependent on another, you've chosen that dependency as your way of life.

You may be in the same place with others or in common situations with others but you are unique. There may be people around you, but they are not *you*. There is the essential *you* that you carry through all your experiences. No one else is ever-present. We alone live in our bodies, with our thoughts and feelings.

No other experience is more private, more alone, than death. Even with loved ones around, a person slips away from the known life into the unknown, alone. She cannot go back and tell others about it; she can't bring someone with her. We know when we die we won't be around to share in the lives of those we care about.

Thoughts of our own death or the death of someone

we depend on for survival or companionship force us to confront our aloneness. We may face the prospect with dread and despair, or we may start to realize that we are able to take care of ourselves.

Much of the resistance to accepting death is demonstrated in our efforts to hold on and cling to others in life. When you must face the death of a loved one, or your own death, it's important to realize that being along and loneliness are not the same thing. To be alone gives you time to think, relax, read, enjoy nature, create, meditate, pray—to appreciate and know yourself. This can enrich and give value to your life. Learning the value of being alone can help you transcend your fears to begin to know and love yourself.

Transcendence is the ability to overcome the primitive fears that we all experience in life, including the fear of being alone. The opportunity to rise above these fears is presented to us occasionally throughout our lives, when major life events related to loss, change and death occur. If we are ready, these experiences can be catalysts, opportunities to move beyond our old patterns of being, and to find inner strength and resources we didn't know we had.

Denial and Hope

It takes courage to face our basic raw emotions, to allow anguish and despair to surface, to confront the sources of our resistances. Yet if we do confront these fears, our own death will be easier.

Most people die the way they lived. If a person has had a pattern of ignoring unpleasant experiences, pretending they never happened, she will handle news of ensuing death the same way. If a person has been explosive and easy to display anger, then he will react in a similar way to the realization of his impending death. If a person has been open and willing to talk about feelings, most likely he or she will handle the dying process the same way.

What is your process? How do you react to bad news, to extreme stress—to change—to disappointment and loss?

Our patterns of reacting to critical life events are established very early in life, probably at birth, and if not raised to a conscious level and altered, they will remain essentially the same. These patterns are called defense mechanisms, or coping styles. They include psychological techniques that protect the person from emotional danger. Sometimes they are effective and sometimes not. Some coping styles are denial, intellectualization, acting-out, projection, displacement, fantasy, repression, dissociation, hypochondriacal behavior, humor and delusions.

The age of the person who is dying has a significant effect on the coping style. For example, young children have not developed the ability to intellectualize, or to use humor, and older people are not rewarded for childish acting-out behavior.

Individual attitudes toward our own life and death change over the years, which affects the way an individual will handle the news of his or her death.

Denial is the first part of the process of dealing with the idea of dying. Death is such a big concept that it is hard to adjust to it all at once. Typically, when one is ill, he has a chance to adjust to a series of smaller losses such as surgery, losing hair with chemotherapy, feeling weaker, incomplete recovery, relapse and returning to the hospital after a time at home. Each time a loss like this occurs, denial is reduced and hope is altered. Denial and hope are partners that keep a dying person going—alive and experiencing feelings—and give time to adjust.

Denial of the reality of one's death protects the psyche from the harshness and pain of giving up life. Hope lets us endure and continue to have a meaningful future, even if the future is shortened. Hope is sustaining. It carries one over and bridges the gap between finding out about your death and accepting it. Hope is the bright light during a time of ambiguity and confusion, protest and bargaining.

You may hope for a scientific breakthrough, a new and complete cure. There may be hope for the tests and the medical reports to be wrong, or to belong to someone else. Sometimes these thoughts are called false hope. They may not be realistic and may be a form of repression, but they buy time to adjust to the idea of dying.

Because we all have plans and goals, it takes readjustment to alter or surrender the future. Gradually, as reality takes over more and more, the achievable goals are realized and the impossible goals given up or changed to ones that can be completed in the time left.

Sometimes having goals keeps us going. As the ragtime pianist and composer Eubie Blake entered his nineties, he received adulation and attention that he had not experienced earlier in his life. Still vigorous in his nineties, he seemed to set living to be one hundred as his goal. His health declined in the last few years, but he reached one hundred, and fans celebrated with concerts and the press covered his birthday. Blake died five days later.

Denial, hope, and acceptance are frequently present at the same time in varying degrees during the initial phases of coming to terms with one's death.

Consider Edna, mother of three small children. She found out that she had terminal cancer when she was thirty-two years old. When she called me from the hospital to tell me the diagnosis, she didn't seem too concerned. She talked of new drugs and other hopeful treatments. Edna was a nurse and knew that the usual survival time was about six months, but *emotionally* she was not ready to accept the facts. She had to work out her internal conflicts.

In the beginning, Edna was in despair about her plans for her children, fussy about their daily habits, clothes, and behavior. At the end, she hardly knew when they were around. She did die within six months. She changed her goals. She settled for being involved in one more birthday instead of a whole lifetime with them. When the birthday (hers) was celebrated, she let go. She accepted her plight, her death. She realized that she must let go of her family and conserve what little energy she had just to survive another day.

For Edna, hope was transformed from clinging and clutching at life to accepting her own end. The night that she died, I was keeping vigil so that her husband could get some rest. She was terribly thin, she had lost so much weight, and she had tumors all over her body. Before her husband left the hospital that evening, she asked me to help her put on some makeup. She said she wanted to look pretty for him because he had been so good to her while she was sick. She died with her makeup on. Hope? Or acceptance? Or reality?

Many who are dying withdraw more and more from involvement in the affairs of everyday life. Hope becomes transformed into faith. We can define hope as desire accompanied by expectation through anticipation, while faith is complete trust and confidence. These two can merge in the final stage of dying for those who have faith that life will go on, that there is life after death or that death is somehow right. As the plans and goals of day-to-day living are shed, expectations change to looking forward to death; to the release from physical pain, withdrawal from the pressures of life.

Self-Awareness

Our understanding of death as a concept changes over our life span. Understanding is an intellectual process. It reaches deeper levels of consciousness by our awareness, belief, experience, and sympathy.

Feelings about death involve emotions such as love, hate, anger, joy and fear. Emotions such as fear are part of our basic survival instinct and serve as warning signs of danger. The fight-or-flight response in animals is part of the alarm system we humans carry with us. If you step out into the street in front of traffic, your body will startle you with a shot of adrenaline, and you will react by jumping to safety. Other emotions like joy and love are connected with empathy, the participation or sharing in the feelings of another.

We all operate our lives from both places—intellect and emotion—but not necessarily in balance. One or the other is usually predominant. Most of the time we are thinking, rational, and predictable in our behavior. Yet if we do not allow the emotional side of ourselves expression, feelings will pile up and often explode in anger, hostility, or violence. Some people hold it all inside and implode, explode inwardly and get sick physically.

Many adults are afraid of and confused by our emotions. We were taught from infancy to control ourselves. Control messages may take the form of: don't get angry . . . big boys don't cry . . . nice girls are reserved and quiet . . . don't act like a tomboy. We learn to deny the feeling side of ourselves at an early age. We are embarrassed if we lose control. The motto for western society is BE STOIC! HOLD IT IN! STAY IN CONTROL! DON'T BE EMOTIONAL!

If we cry or act angry, joyful, or happy we are not sure how others will respond. One reason adults lose the ability to be playful and have fun is that we were taught to deny emotional expression. Emotions, in fact, are neither good nor bad. They just are. They are part of all of us. Some are pleasant and some are unpleasant. The emotional part of grieving and mourning is prolonged and more difficult for people who learned to be stoic and cut themselves off from their feelings.

You can learn to recognize your emotions. Here's one way. Anytime that you feel a strong negative reaction to a person, place or thing, your emotional side is giving you a clue that you have some unresolved issues that need attention. If you stop and take the time to analyze what happened, recognize and identify your feelings, you will be able to begin to resolve that particular problem for yourself.

It's rewarding to reclaim and make friends with the emotional side of yourself. Do not deny and be afraid of your emotions; acknowledge and respect them. They are an important part of you. Accepting our feelings as well as our intellect helps us to be balanced human beings.

As we integrate our emotions with our intellect, we become more *self-aware*, more *self-conscious*. It is like turning on a light using a rheostat, a switch which gradually regulates the brightness or dimness of an electric light. The older we are, the more time and experiences we have had. Time gives us the potential to be advanced in awareness, and gradually our light can shine brighter, so that by old age we will have accepted death as the next and final uncompleted task in life. Learning from life and being attuned to our reactions are the way we achieve self-awareness, enlightenment.

Age at Death

An infant or retarded person has a very dim light— little self-awareness. Knowledge of or emotional attachment to their lives is minimal or nonexistent.

A pre-school child imagines death primarily as a separation from her parents. She fears losing them, and she fears going to a hospital. These fears are more real than the fear of death. With some explanation, she may come to think of death as being like a long sleep or going to see God—which she imagines as an extension of her parents, an authority figure.

At age six to twelve, death is still a fantasy, distant and unreal. If a child this age has been told he will die, he may misbehave or complain of every little ache and pain to get attention and the reassurance that he is loved and won't be abandoned. The child has become involved with people outside the family but hasn't much concept of the future. Death may be seen as an interruption of achievements—"But I've just learned to ride my bike"—or a disruption of friendships.

These children should continue with normal activities like school, sports and hobbies, and with friendships as long as possible. Those are the important issues in this age group.

In adolescence, there's a growing sense of identity and the uniqueness of "me" as an individual. A teenager who is dying may feel that knowing she is valuable, has a special identity and worth, is the most important feeling to embrace.

Adolescents still don't have a sense of living for a long time, even though they're beginning to plan for the future. That's why young people make the best soldiers: they're strong, daring, willing to risk their lives for glory and adventure and recognition.

This is the time of life when peer group is important. They care about what their friends think of them. Physical image is also important, and the bodily changes that result from illness may be especially difficult at this age.

The adolescent facing death should stay in touch with friends as much as possible. Acceptance and love from his peers and social status may be more important to him than his parents. The adolescent's tendency to veer wildly from mature self-sufficiency to childlike vulnerability will be more extreme in the stress of serious illness.

One young man, seventeen years old, was on his school's football team when he found out that he had leukemia. He practiced with the team as long as possible, played in the first game of the season, and died before the season ended. As he adjusted to the idea of his death, his biggest concern was what his friends thought of him. He worried about letting the team down. The entire football team, including the coach and cheerleaders, visited him in the hospital. They reassured him that he was important to them. He died feeling validated in the way that mattered most to him.

In early adulthood, news of fatal illness is understandably met with outrage and fury. "It isn't fair," "I'm just getting started in life," "Not me . . . not now." The light of self-awareness is getting brighter only to be snuffed out prematurely. There is so much to do and not enough time. Relationships may be fewer than in adolescence, but they are better in quality and importance. Family and a few special friends are the main sources of psychological support.

An adult under forty will greet death with severe feelings of disappointment, anger, and frustration. It's unfair. There is so much to *do*, because at this stage of life, we prove our worth by doing—being *involved* in politics, or community groups, working, having children, going to P.T.A. or Little League meetings, traveling, learning, achieving in our work.

Young adults must shorten goals and expectations for their life. They will have to settle for another birthday as Edna did or one more holiday spent with the family. The final time can be lived to the fullest but the future is only tomorrow.

After forty, news of impending death may be somewhat more acceptable. Middle-age, roughly forty to sixty-five years, is the time of life to enjoy the benefits of the work of the past years. Sometime during the forties, many people experience another identity crisis similar to adolescence, as they face changes in physical appearance, a decline in stamina, status, and possibly reduced sexual interest. Sometimes it is a time to turn inward and to evaluate life's goals and work, to consider the quality of life instead of quantity. Time perspective changes also, and people begin to think about the number of years left to live, instead of the number of years since birth.

It is during the middle years that most people bury their parents and become the "older" generation in their families. Companionship becomes more important in relationships than sex, and new depth of sharing and understanding in marriage may result. Adjustment in the middle years may involve learning to shift from physically-based values to wisdom-based values, and finding new and creative solutions to current and future problems.

It is also the time when the nest empties. Children leave home and parents can live without the demands and pressures of children. In these years, there's a high incidence of divorce, but the marriages that make it through become better than ever. Men generally become more gentle and sensitive, and women become more assertive.

Many of life's tasks have been completed, yet these years are still active and productive. Death means that careers will be interrupted and loving relationships with spouses, children, grandchildren, and friends will be cut short. Death denies a person a chance to harvest the fruits of one's labors, develop leisure interests and to travel, enjoy retirement and grandchildren and family. Death now ends life before it is finished, like a thief.

Some of us are able to regard death during the middle years from a more philosophical position— thinking of the meaning of life and death, evaluating whether your life has had value to yourself and others.

In advanced adulthood, one is aware that death is closer. In the sixties, we reevaluate setting new goals and ways to use time. We may believe that living past sixty-five years is a bonus. Only a few decades ago the average life span was much shorter: fifty-two for women and forty-eight for men. Now women live to seventy-two years, and men to sixty-eight years on the average. Many people live past the end of their work life.

In old age, one reviews one's life and may feel satisfied that it has been worthwhile or may try to repair former failures.

Death now is less feared, sometimes even anticipated with interest. In the case of poor health or chronic illness, death may be strongly welcomed. If life has been a disappointment, then death will be less acceptable until some of the problems of one's life have been resolved.

On the other hand, old age and retirement can be the most delightful time of life, full of peace, happiness, and contentment. In such cases, though one may hate to go, death is more readily accepted as a natural part of the life cycle. Most elderly people who truly fear death have not yet made peace with themselves. When a life has been fulfilling and had an impact on others, the light of this life can reach its peak of brightness, then flicker and, like a shooting star, streak across the sky in a final blaze of glory.

Other Fears: How You Die

For many, the fear of death focuses on how you will die. Worries about physical deterioration and appearance, pain, panic, and dying alone or in an institution, can preoccupy your thoughts and delay coming to terms with death.

A friend of mine with a severe chronic lung problem partially accepted the inevitable prospect of her death but would panic at the thought of suffocating. She often said that she had come to terms with the fact that she was dying, but she wished it were over. Her fear was in *how* she would die. She prayed for her end to come in her sleep or in a merciful coma.

Specific personal fears will be of great concern during the time when you are told the nature and extent of your illness. In the beginning when you first acknowledge symptoms such as a tumor, pain, or unusual bleeding, you most likely also experienced a psychological fear about the nature and extent of the physical problem. Maybe all the facts were unknown and unconfirmed at that point in time. When you were told the results and probable outcome of your disease after diagnostic tests or surgery, you may have felt relief at knowing the truth. Yet feelings of numbness, shock, disbelief, great anguish, and fear also might be present at the moment of truth.

Final Decisions

The crisis of knowing that you are going to die creates a need to rearrange life plans, goals, activities, and relationships. Dealing with your own death is a new learning process, perhaps the most important one so far. You are forced to reevaluate and relearn something important . . . how to live and how to die.

At first the news will elicit feelings of anger, fear, doubt, dread, insecurity, confusion, rage, disappointment and many other feelings. After a while your old barriers and defenses will crumble. Then you will begin to talk and make decisions that will affect you and your loved ones who will survive your death.

Deciding on the disposal of your body after death can be difficult. Burial or cremation may seem dismal or unthinkable prospects. The thought of an autopsy, or donating useful organs to other people, may be morbid and painful. These concerns may be partly related to the denial of your death, and partly related to the fear of non-being.

After physical death our bodies quickly begin to break down, just as any organic matter does. We no longer can experience sensations. Yet when we think about the choices of burial or cremation, and choose "none of the above," we are projecting fears and feelings onto our bodies past their usefulness to us.

The sooner these issues are worked through and resolved, the better. You may choose to ignore or avoid making decisions about your burial for yourself, but open and frank discussion of your wishes with your next of kin or closest friends will do a great deal to relieve everyone of these worries.

Dealing with knowledge of your death involves facing the fears of letting go of life as you have known it and lived it so far. It is time to make decisions, to resolve problems, to make amends, and to clean up outstanding issues in relationships. This gift of time between knowing about your death and when you actually die may be used in a beneficial way for yourself and for others to complete your financial affairs, resolve unfinished conflicts, and say goodbye with love.

The only way to prepare for sudden, accidental or unexpected death is to realize that we are all vulnerable to death. Make a will, discuss burial plans and financial issues with your family. Regularly keep them informed about changes in life insurance benefits, pensions and keys to your safe deposit box.

Death is a difficult enough crisis to survive without having to cope with such problems.

Settle important issues as rapidly as you can— financial affairs that affect those who survive you, problems in relationships, and questions about your life's priorities. You can't be guaranteed a future, since no one can be fully protected against death or tragedy. But having the loose ends of your life tied up as much as possible makes today, as well as tomorrow, more fulfilling and content.

The Roman philosopher Seneca said, "Unlike life, death cannot be taken away from man, and therefore we may consider it is *the* gift of God."

RICHARD CORY

Whenever Richard Cory went down town
  We people on the pavement looked at him;
He was a gentleman from sole to crown,
  Clean favored, and imperially slim.

And he was always quietly arrayed,
  And he was always human when he talked;
But still he fluttered pulses when he said,
  "Good-morning," and he glittered when he walked.

And he was rich—yes, richer than a king,
  And admirably schooled in every grace;
In fine, we thought that he was everything
  To make us wish that we were in his place.

So on we worked, and waited for the light,
  And went without the meat, and cursed the bread;
And Richard Cory, one calm summer night,
  Went home and put a bullet through his head.

                              Edwin Arlington Robinson

CHAPTER TEN

DEATH BY SUICIDE

Martha wept as she told about her son, John. He visited her a week before he hanged himself. The night before he was to return to his city, he put his arm around his mother and told her that he loved her, and that she had been a good mother to him. All of this was unusual because he had never been demonstrative before, she said. She thought that he was changing for the better. Earlier in the day he had commented jokingly that he wouldn't be around to enjoy a family party planned for two weeks later. His mother took that to mean that he would be back at his home. After his death, she was able to piece together the hidden meaning in what he was saying.

What bothered her most was that John had left a will disposing of all his property, his apartment was immaculate, he had on his best clothes, and he had written out checks to all his creditors. On the checks to the utility companies, he filled in their names, put "FINAL BILL," and left the amount blank.

His mother said that John was quiet and unassuming, never any trouble to anyone . . . a *loner*. He was the same way in death. How consistent we are.

Psychologically, this twenty-five-year-old young man

is almost a classic case. He lived by himself in a city away from his only support system, his family, and was a *loner*. He lived in San Francisco, the city with the highest suicide rate in the country. He had completed a bachelor's degree in college and had a good technical job with a national company. He had a new car, a nice apartment, and plenty of money. He had achieved all that life held for him, but he was still not fulfilled or happy. He was empty. The American Dream had failed him—or he had failed it. He had it all and yet he had nothing. He was white, male and single—all high risk factors for suicide. He had no friends.

The lack of contact with other human beings was probably the single most critical fact. Successes in life are often meaningless if they are not shared with others. His lifetime pattern of extreme introversion indicated a prevailing feeling of worthlessness and insecurity in relationships. Perhaps the few times he tried to reach out to others in his life for friendship, he was rebuffed and gave up too easily, only to feel more isolated and without value. Possibly the problem was that he simply lacked social skills. Yet he expected to be rejected and created situations where this would happen. His worthlessness was validated.

What was there to live for? He had few memories of past happiness and satisfaction, even though he did the things that are supposed to make people happy. He had an education, a good job, and the material accoutrements to signal to others that he was successful. With no satisfaction in the present, the feelings of emptiness continued. For someone like John, the loneliness continues, if there are no friends. No one cares if you live or die. No one to miss you—no one to grieve. No difference in the world with or without you.

And finally, he had no *hope*. No hope of anything different, no expectation of satisfaction in the future.

With no past, no present, no future, there was no reason to live.

John was a bright young man. He made his decision based on the evidence. And in the post-decision euphoria he cleaned up his life. He said his goodbyes, gave away his possessions, and paid his bills. "He was never any trouble to anybody," his mother told me. But she was wrong. And he was wrong to feel that no one cared. Now his mother cries, and his father can't; they wonder what went wrong.

Guilt and Regrets

The word "survive" comes from two Latin words *super*, which means over, and *vivere*, which means to live. If someone you have loved and been involved with commits suicide, they have left you behind to survive. As a survivor you must, then, go on and start over *to live* again.

If the suicide came as a shock and surprise, your grieving process will be doubly difficult. Probably the most powerful and hostile rejection a person can make of another is to commit suicide. To the survivor, the death seems like a photograph, a flat, two-dimensional image of an incident. Many people can look at the image and relate to parts of it, but no one person can know or understand all dimensions of the event totally. During the grieving process it is necessary to come to terms with the past issues, stresses, and problems remaining from the relationship with the suicidee. Because there are always so many questions left unanswered, this can be a very difficult and painful experience.

Every person who has been involved with the suicidee will be forced to examine himself for his part, and all may feel some guilt, responsibility, and self-blame. It is especially difficult for the spouse or parents of the suicidee. Grieving follows the same general process as in other deaths, but guilt prolongs recovery.

When a person is planning to kill himself, he often gives clues to friends and family members by dropping subtle hints. Many friends and family members either do not choose to believe, or do not understand, the message being given. Often friends have heard the threats or complaints before.

Even if they do hear the message loud and clear, they may not know what to do about it or to whom they can turn for help. They wonder how to prevent the suicide but feel powerless to stop it. Often they deny to themselves and others that such a thing could actually happen, and later the denial is a source of a great deal of guilt and self-blame.

Even though there may have been signals and warning signs prior to the suicide, you could not realize the impact that the actual death would inflict upon you. The suicide of a family member is a triple threat. It is a sudden death, with no time to prepare for your grief. It is the loss of a significant person in your life, and it is an action loaded with emotional content.

You will experience grief over a suicide in the same identifiable stages. In the beginning you will feel shock, numbness and disbelief. This will last beyond the funeral, possibly up to two weeks.

There is a danger during these first weeks of immersing yourself in denial and repression. But to repress or subdue or restrain any painful thoughts or feelings can delay your natural grieving process. It is crucial that you allow the emotions that come to you to be expressed. If you do not grieve now, you will have to do so later and may develop neurotic and/or phobic symptoms as a result, even years after the event.

The funeral is a time to get support from family, friends, and others who may share the pain and anguish of the death. It is an important time to begin to realize the truth of the situation. The funeral is the ritual of separation. It is for you, the living. It is both public and personal acknowledgment of the end of the deceased's life. It's your chance to begin to say goodbye, to begin to let go, to start the rest of your life—as a survivor.

Even if you allow yourself to do the work of grieving as it presents itself to you, it will probably take from one to two years before you feel normal again. It will seem difficult, even impossible, to reestablish an interest in living your life with joy and happiness.

Working through your grief will release you from the bondage of your relationship with the dead person. You have a right to survive. You can survive. And you will have a new strength and value that you never imagined possible. While the pain you will feel will be hell for a while, it can be a gift in disguise—a gift for growth—for a new way of being. George Eliot said, "The strongest principle of growth lies in human choice." *You have a choice*.

After the initial period of shock, bewilderment, and denial, another phase will slowly begin to take over. As the numbness wears off, the reality of the death will creep more and more into your awareness. Your thoughts are likely to be on the dead person. Confusion will prevail. You may feel a certain amount of relief at being out of a "bad" relationship, if there were problems. Now is the time to be glad that the problems are over. Try to do this without guilt or self-blame. Everyone wishes for release from the trials in life from time to time.

You may be uptight about your relationship being held up to public scrutiny. Suicide has a way of exposing private matters to questioning and speculation by others. You may be worried about what others are thinking or saying about you. Try to forget this. It will only prolong your grieving. If people like you, they will not judge you. People who are not sympathetic to you will not believe any defense you make. It is impossible for everyone to accept and approve of you. Seek your true friends.

Your job now is to survive, not to defend yourself to others. Ask someone you trust to be with you when you feel like talking or crying. If you think others blame you for the death, talk it out, cry it out. Some of what you may think others are saying about you may be a projection of what you deeply feel or fear about yourself. If this is so, then it is time for you to get in touch with these thoughts and feelings. Only by bringing them to the surface can you release yourself from them.

This will be a time to break the old habits of the relationship. You can help speed up the process by getting rid of as many reminders as possible, such as clothes, toys, and other pieces of personal property. Rearrange the furniture, or paint and redecorate the room; use it for another purpose. Move into another bedroom, another bed in the house if you slept with that person. Don't destroy all reminders of the person like photographs or special mementos; just put them away for a while. There were good times that you will want to remember later and share with others.

Memorializing the dead loved one is unhealthy and is a form of denial of the reality of the death. To get on with your own life, it is important to get ready to let go of the other person. You must bury him/her psychologically as well as physically. Keeping personal belongings or setting aside a room as a monument or going to the grave site every day will only prolong your pain and your grief.

During this early time of adjustment there will be difficult issues for you to handle. The police and coroner's office may insist that you attend a public hearing to officially declare the death a suicide. In dealing with insurance agents, you may find that your policy will pay less or nothing in the case of suicide.

If there is a suicide note, you will have to decide what

to do with it. The police may have it for a time. Later, keeping it may be a problem, another connection and reminder of this traumatic part in your life. Putting it away in a safety deposit box may be a good idea until you are ready to destroy it. Better yet, a ceremonial burning will release you of the problem and serves as a symbol of letting go.

Another difficult issue is how to handle the suicide publicly. Because suicide provokes negative responses from people in general, it is tempting to lie when talking to strangers or people remotely involved in your life. Protect yourself in any way that feels right for you at the time. If it is easier to evade the question than to feel defensive, do so. A lie may catch up with you at some later date, but you don't have to share the details with everyone. One suggestion is simply to say that the event is too close to you and that you would rather not talk about it right now.

My father committed suicide when I was twenty-three years old. For many years I was so ashamed of this that I vowed to never tell my children about the way their grandfather died. I lived in another state and it was easy to hide the fact of his suicide from anyone who might tell them in the future. I never talked about it to friends. I swore my husband to secrecy. For years I lived in the fear that if my children ever found out the truth, it would harm them or the way they felt about me and my family. I wanted them to love their grandfather, even though he died before they were born. As they grew up I knew they would want to hear stories about their grandfather, and I wanted only good stories to be remembered. Suicide is not a good story.

Finally, after ten or twelve years of my hiding the truth, I told them about his death. To my surprise, they were very nonchalant and unconcerned about the whole thing. It did not destroy them for life, and they could love him for all of what they knew about both his

life and death. I realized then that the secret was not
really for their sake, but for mine. I had been ashamed
of myself. I felt hurt and angry and guilty. I felt rejected
and abandoned, and I did not know what to do with
these painful feelings, so I buried them inside myself
until I was forced to face them. I was really protecting
myself from accepting the truth of his death.

Guilt is the most difficult emotion to confront. No
doubt you will mentally go over and over the events of
the person's last day, and the days and weeks prior to
the death—trying to make sense of the whole thing,
searching for answers, asking questions that will never
be answered or verified because the only person who
can answer them is dead. You will ask, "Why did he do
it?"; "Why did she do this to me?"; "Why didn't she tell
me things were so bad?"; "Why didn't he trust me to
love and help him?"; "Didn't she think of the problems
this would cause for us?"; and "Why didn't he pay the
last premium of the insurance policy?"; "Why couldn't I
stop him?"; "What did I do wrong?"; "Didn't I love her
enough?"; "I should have done something." These and
many other questions will haunt you if you let them.
Don't dwell on them because there are no answers now,
only more crazy-making questions.

Guilt comes from a feeling of regret or remorse,
believing that you have either done something wrong
that you wish you had not done, or from failing to do
something you think you should have done. You can
spend years going over every argument, every nasty
word, every conversation, and punish yourself for what
you should have done or should have said that might
have made a difference. But remorse accomplishes nothing except making you feel worse.

When you feel guilty, you also feel that you are to
blame and that you *should* be punished, as if you have
committed a crime. We lock criminals away from the rest
of society. But no one is going to punish you or lock you

away except yourself. And this is not necessary. Guilt is completely unproductive. It will only delay your recovery. Of course it is great for dragging out a desire for self-pity, and any self-destructive feelings or wishes you may have for yourself.

You may feel both relieved and sorry that you are alive and the other person is not. All of these ambivalent feelings are normal and a natural response to this tragedy in your life.

The truth is that whatever happened in the past—*you did the best that you could at the time*. Now forgive yourself! And then you can begin to get on with your life. If you do not do this—you are continuing to give the memory of your dead loved one all the power over your present life.

Closely connected with guilt are feelings of failure. You may think that you have failed as a friend, as a parent, spouse, or child but, mostly, as a human being. You may berate yourself for not being more sensitive to the signals, for not preventing the suicide, for not knowing the seriousness of the threat. Or in anger you may have said something like, "You keep threatening to kill yourself. Why don't you just go ahead and get it over with?"

You may be searching your soul for your responsibility in the death. Blaming yourself directly or indirectly for causing it. Don't worry. These thoughts and feelings are normal and common. In time they will pass. Focus on being gentle and kind to yourself.

Survival Techniques

The period from about three months to one year after the death will be an intense period of emotional turmoil and confusion. One day or even one minute you may feel relieved, even euphoric; then you may begin to cry, then feel angry and hostile, depressed and sad. All of these emotions will flood over you. This is a time to be extremely gentle and good to yourself. Allow the emotions to come out and to be expressed. If you do, they will spend themselves and pass sooner.

The next stage you will probably go through will include some feelings of depression and anger. The confusion will begin to clear. Depression comes with the realization that the death really happened. It happened the way it did. And it is final and irreversible. Depression is anger turned inward. You will feel powerless and impotent. There will probably be lingering feelings of guilt and failure that need to be worked through.

Symptoms of depression include sleep problems, listlessness, low energy level, fatigue, decreased interest in sex, poor appetite or eating all the time, feeling low down or sad. There are some anti-depressant drugs on the market which your physician can prescribe for you. They will buy you some time that you may need for the healing process. Recovery is really a matter of time passing and allowing yourself to do the necessary grief work to get through the process of grieving.

Do not take drugs for your depression if you can possibly get along without them. Like alcohol and tranquilizers, they are a crutch. You will get through your grief faster if you are fully aware. Occasionally you may choose something to help you relax and sleep. Anti-depressants must be taken for several months to be fully effective, and some have unfavorable side effects. If you do think you would like to take them for a while, read all you can about them, especially the one prescribed for you. You can go to the library and look up any drug in a book called the *P.D.R. (Physician's Desk Reference)*. Doctors use this book all the time. It has information about dosages, manufacturers of the drug, side effects and contraindications.

After all, it is your body and you should make an informed decision about taking any drug for a long time.

f your doctor has problems with you being informed bout your medication, get another doctor. Your doctor s only your employee. He or she should be a consultant o you—not a god.

Other effective non-drug ways to handle stress are xercise, massage, spa facilities (i.e. steam room, acuzzi, and swimming pools); and body-work pro-grams such as polarity and reflexology or aerobic exer-ise classes.

The length of time you will be depressed will depend on the amount of resistance that you have to feeling the necessary sadness, disappointment, and anger that you have seething inside of you.

Here is an exercise that may help you look at your resistance. Lie down in a quiet place. Relax. Let's try ome imagery. Think of resistance as a powerful force against which you stand firm, unyielding, and in oppo-sition. Imagine a door that someone is trying to open rom the other side. You have a great fear of whatever is on the other side of that door. So, with all of your might you push and push to keep that door closed. You may even feel terror and panic if the door opens even a crack. You don't really *know* what is on the other side, but you *think* that it must be bad. You must constantly be vigilant or the door will open. You resist facing your own feelings. How exhausting!

Now, go to the door and try holding it closed with all of your strength. Have someone push to try to open it. Pay attention to your body, to where you hold tension, to the stress and strain of resisting. Pay attention to the focus of your mind, to your thoughts. They are involved with the single purpose of keeping the door closed. After a while you don't have the strength to hold it any longer. Your resistance is gone now, you will have to open the door, look at whatever is on the other side, look at your pain and anger and fears.

Imagine that you stop resisting and you open the door

a little. What is there? Look at it . . . listen to it . .
feel it. It is part of you. Own it. Take it inside. It's okay
you can handle your feelings. Open the door a little at a
time. Let in some light (enlightenment), and some fresh
air (new ways of being). They do not have to be your
own private bogeymen, your own private hell!

Sometime it is necessary to go to the depths of despair
to really know that *you are a survivor*. When you do this
and come back, you know that you will make it.

It is better to be resilient than resistant. But in order to
be resilient, to spring back to your original form, you
must stop resisting. The sooner you open the door, the
sooner you will release the emotional charge of those
painful feelings. Anger is often the most frightening
feeling.

Anger at yourself comes from guilt, shame and self-
blame. If you are stuck here and feel the need to be
punished, you may be in trouble with self-destructive
desires of your own. Get help! These thoughts are
common, but they mustn't become more than thoughts.
All your family needs now is another suicide!

When the Suicidee Is a Spouse

When I asked a client recently about his feelings of
anger toward his wife who had shot herself eleven
months ago, he said, "Of course I'm not mad at her. She
tried to tell me the night before and I didn't understand.
If I had only taken more time to listen to her, she might
still be alive today and I wouldn't be here now." He was
still struggling with guilt and self-blame. In time, I hope
he will move beyond these feelings to get on with his
life. He will have to acknowledge that his wife's death
created chaos in his life and in the lives of their children.
He has many reasons to feel angry at her, but he isn't
aware of these feelings yet.

Another client raged three months after her husband's death, "I am furious at Harry! How could he leave me like this? I have two kids to raise that I really didn't want in the first place. I had them because *he* wanted kids. He didn't pay the last premium on the insurance policy, and I don't know how I am going to survive financially." At least she can admit her anger and the source of it . . . her dead husband Harry. Her progress is in the right direction, but she still has to learn what to do with anger and how to let it go and finally to forgive Harry and to release him.

Eventually you will think less about the never-to-be-answered questions. You will not continually dwell on her or him; in fact, soon little of your thinking will be about that event in your life. You will begin to experience pleasure again, alone and with others.

When you can say, "You are dead and I am alive. I release you from my life with love, and now it is time for me to get on with the rest of my life"—then you will know you are better.

Releasing him doesn't mean completely erasing the memories of this relationship from your existence. This person and this death are part of your life experience. You may continue to feel twinges of regret and sadness, especially at significant times, like anniversaries. This is normal and to be expected. What is not normal is being so occupied with the memory of the person and the suicide that it continues to interfere with your life after a "reasonable" period of time. A reasonable period of time is between one and two years, with slow progress being made along the way.

Your reaction to the suicide of a loved one, just as your reaction to any other death or major loss, will depend on several factors. These include your personality, the events surrounding the death, the way you have dealt with change and grief in the past, and your relationship with your loved one.

After a suicide, the surviving spouse is often left with

a deep sense of failure and confusion, especially when an impulsive or planned suicide is a gesture of anger or hostility, directed at you.

One woman killed herself on her husband's birthday wearing the locket that he had given her as a birthday present. He didn't understand why she did it. He felt that he should have known and been able to prevent her death. Obviously her act was in anger and rejection of him. She wanted to hurt him, and she succeeded.

Socially, the widow or widower of a suicidee is more likely to be shunned than to get support from friends and other widows or widowers. He or she is also more likely to feel abandoned and/or rejected. Additional stress may develop from in-laws casting blame for the death.

If you have children, especially young ones, you will have the added burden of helping them through their grief, and resolving conflicts and guilt that they may have. If possible, find a family member or friend to act as a confidante and support system for each child. Someone they can trust and talk to openly will help you and your children.

Tell their teachers the situation so they can be patient and on the lookout for problems that might surface in school. Don't abdicate your role as a parent, but for a while you will be so preoccupied with your own grief that it will be difficult for you to take good care of the needs of others.

You need all the help you can get. Don't hesitate to ask for the help. Because if you don't let people know you need help, they may be hesitant to offer it, thinking they are interfering. It is up to you to recognize that you need help and to find it. You may not always get it the first time you ask, or from the people you think should respond to your needs. Don't be discouraged. Try again. Be specific about the help that will be best for you and ask for it. Find someone to clean the house, or someone to be a substitute parent for your children for a while, or someone to stay with you at night when you can't bear being alone. Ask for whatever you want or need.

When the Suicidee Is a Parent

Young children of a person who commits suicide will have unique issues to deal with. Because their parents are so crucial in their lives, they may be unable to see factors outside themselves as being important to their parents. So they may believe they're responsible for the suicide because they are "bad" or unlovable children. Or they may recall a time when the dead parent was angry with them. They may feel that they "cost" too much if they asked for toys or food while shopping with the parent.

They may have been angry at the parent for some punishment and have wished that the parent was either dead or would go away "forever." In this case especially, they may feel that they caused the death. As a result, they may develop a great fear of their own power over life and death. They may have told the parent that they hated him, or even had such a thought, and feel terribly guilty after the death.

It is extremely important for the child to be able to remember these incidents and to talk about them in order to release them, and understand that he's not responsible for the parent's death. Otherwise, they may lie hidden for a long time and fester, finally erupting years later in behavior that is self-punishing.

Children must be reassured that negative feelings toward parents are sometimes perfectly normal and that such feelings do not cause people to kill themselves.

They must learn that the suicidee—and no one else— made the decision to die for her own reasons. Because of the death, children will feel abandoned and rejected by the death. If the child is insecure about being lovable, those feelings will be reinforced by a parent's suicide. It may take a lot of time and patience and professional help to reassure the child that he is valued and worthwhile.

If the child is denying her feelings in the death, she may blame someone else in the family for the death—often the living parent. This of course is a difficult problem for the entire family. It may be necessary to get outside professional help to clean up the relationships.

Like the surviving spouse, children often feel that they should or could have been able to prevent the suicide. They may think that rescue attempts should have been more effective to reverse the death and to save the parent. The image of the dead parent may haunt them for years in dreams and daydreams, especially if the death was a violent one or if they saw the body.

The age of the child at the time of the death will make a difference in memories, guilt, fears and overall effects. Every child will have issues to deal with before he is free of trauma and stigma of a parental suicide.

If a child strongly identified with the parent, it is likely that he will have suicide fantasies of his own, especially as he approaches the same age as that of the parent who died. Such children—even as adults—may fear and, at the same time, entertain thoughts of ending their own life in a similar way.

Phobias may develop that are closely related to the death of the parent, such as a fear of guns, drugs, or heights. Sometimes physical symptoms develop that are similar to the way a parent died, like getting choking feelings if the parent hanged himself, or trouble breathing if the parent inhaled lethal fumes.

Rosalie, a client of mine, started to prepare a will and to plan for the distribution of her property at the age of thirty-one. Her activity was compulsive rather than planned. She didn't know why she was doing it, but she felt that she had to. For about six months before her thirty-second birthday, she grew increasingly restless, and thought off and on about how her family would get along without her. She occasionally had thoughts about being dead. She didn't consciously plan or think about killing herself.

As her birthday approached, she had an anxiety attack full of panic and confused, undefined fears. In exploring her past, she revealed that her mother committed suicide at the age of thirty-two. Subconsciously, she thought she would end her life in the same way. When she was able to bring the hidden fears to the surface and handle them, she was extremely relieved to reach her thirty-second birthday.

When the Suicidee Is a Child

The parents of a child who kills himself live with a profound sense of failure as well as feelings of guilt. They blame themselves and each other for the death. I recently heard of a thirteen-year-old boy who hanged himself. Next to his body was the report card that he got at school that day. He had received a D grade in one subject and couldn't face the disapproval of his father, who encouraged and expected excellence in his son. A brief note said, "Dad, I'm sorry I let you down."

If the child is an adult, the parents may project blame onto others such as demands of college, the job, or a wife or husband.

Surviving children are sometimes encouraged to take the place of the dead one: "Well, John got into a good college, you can too." The surviving child may be identified with the deceased one: "You hold your fork just like John did." Sometimes the child is seen as a hero: "It takes a lot of guts to knock yourself off." Occasionally families will try to make reparation by giving money to a worthy cause like a suicide prevention program, or to a student counseling service in a college.

One of the biggest tragedies is that such a death often drives a wedge into family relationships instead of bringing people together. Everyone in a family suffers over any death, but death by self-destruction is even more difficult to understand and come to terms with.

I encourage you to turn to those relationships that are closest to you for support. Talk together; cry and mourn together. Compare feelings, reactions, anger and frustration. So often family members withdraw into themselves or go their separate ways when tragedy strikes instead of sharing the grief and supporting each other. It is easier to work out your feelings of guilt, failure, and blame with loving support.

Forgive and begin to live again. Don't run away from your pain or from your loved ones. This is the time that you really need each other. Risk reaching out and asking for the love and care that you need now, and be available to give the same loving and caring to others. Get beneath the surface of reliving the details and talk about your feelings, fears, and frustrations.

For a while, survival will be just an effort to get through one day at a time. Some days will be better than others. Slowly, gradually, time will pass and you will heal. Be good to yourself. Be kind to yourself. You have more to do in life, and you must survive to do it.

The Mystery of Suicide

Most suicides result from a combination of factors. When someone has had enough of life, it's difficult to identify any one reason for death. Sometimes a change can be a crisis event that precipitates suicidal behavior. Such potentially dangerous events might be the threat or actual loss of a loved one through death; separation or divorce; changes in self-image such as in an accident or rape or beating; loss of a job; sudden illnesses and hospitalization; loss of motivation or energy to start over or to renew the missing part of one's life.

Most people have thought of suicide at least once in their lifetime. But why do we all think about it and only few of us do it? For those who attempt and/or complete suicide, the big difference is that they have closed the gap in the thinking process. That is, they actually see themselves as dead now, not in the future. They see their lives as already over, and the actual death is an "after the fact" action.

Suicide presents more questions than answers, especially for the survivor trying to understand the puzzle of a suicide. It is complicated and frightening. Probably no one who has not seriously attempted suicide can fully understand why someone would go through with it, but there are some common patterns.

It's when whatever is most important in one's life seems to be missing, destroyed or unattainable that life seems no longer worth the effort. Why go on living when there is more pain than pleasure? There are feelings of helplessness and powerlessness. Perhaps anger turned inward.

Depression plays an important part in suicide. Many suicides are committed just before or while a person is coming out of a depression.

When no single event seems to be the trigger, there probably has been a long period of depression or dissatisfaction with something crucial.

Before the decision to kill oneself, most people go through a crisis in problem solving. During this process there is an increase of tension and confusion as solutions continue to be elusive. More feelings of disorganization and the inability to sort out positive solutions and choices for the future lead to greater levels of frustration and confusion. The lack of success in resolving the tension with familiar problem-solving techniques leads to helplessness and hopelessness.

When the problem continues, the person may see death as the only way out of the dilemma. The state of prolonged tension may last a few hours to a few months or longer. It may be combined with other emotional reactions such as anxiety, chaos, panic, sadness, a sense of loss, depression, denial and repression of thoughts and feelings, excessive fantasies, hope for a better life on a spiritual plane, or a sense of deprivation.

If the feelings of isolation and worthlessness continue with no visible hope or sign of things getting better, suicide may be the result. In the worst moments of despair, the person feels totally alone and has no sense of identity or worth. "No one understands me. No one loves me. No one ever will, because I am unlovable."

Suicide has been called the ultimate cry for help! It is also the ultimate act of anger. It is the final rejection and punishment of oneself, society and all others concerned. The threat of suicide can be used as a tool for manipulation. Death by suicide can have incredible power over the lives of the survivors. Family, relatives, friends, neighbors, co-workers, boss, and others are left with pain, confusion, and sometimes guilt over the death. They have no choice except to live with their grief and all of their unanswered questions.

Ambivalence characterizes the thoughts of those contemplating suicide. They want both to live and to die, to be out of their present misery and pain, and sometimes to punish those whom they think caused it. These mixed motivations are seen in the suicide notes that express both love and hate, anger and regret, fear and hopelessness.

These opposing impulses to live and die often are expressed in suicide attempts. Someone swallows a bottle of pills, then calls for help before going unconscious. However, if a person acts self-destructively during agitation or under the influence of alcohol or drugs, there may be a sense of unreality to the event and a call for help may not come, or may be too late.

When an act is impulsive, especially in anger, one doesn't fully think through the reality of the consequence. Rather the desire for revenge or a wish to induce guilt in another person is the motive, and it is accompanied with a reckless disregard for the finality of death for one's self.

Some people take their lives rather than go through a terminal disease. They are trying to avoid pain or do not wish to burden their families with the expense and grief of watching them die a slow death. Many elderly suicidees feel that death is preferable to the physical deterioration, isolation, and loneliness that are so often dreaded by those who have outlived family and friends. Living out their final days in a nursing home is not a pleasant choice. Making a rational decision about when and how to die is a preferable option.

For some people, suicide is a well-thought-out, rational decision. For others, it is a reaction to incredible stress, fear and depression—an act of desperation. Perhaps in the first instance it is truly a choice to exercise the right to make a decision about one's own life. In the second, it is not a rational "action," but a "reaction" to intolerable circumstances currently operating in the life of a person.

Almost every town in the United States has a crisis intervention center where a person who is feeling desperate can call and talk to caring people. These people are trained to talk to those who are thinking about suicide. If you or someone close to you is talking about suicide or giving verbal or non-verbal clues about self-destruction, contact your local HELP LINE or Suicide Prevention Service (names vary from city to city). They can refer you to competent counseling, talk you through the immediate crisis, or console a family member. For the suicidal individual, it is important to restore hope and a sense of worth, and to recall former times of strength and hope.

The Living Will

For those who are chronically ill, the Living Will is an aid to death with dignity without extensive medical intervention to extend life beyond the time a natural death would occur. It allows a person to maintain some control over death. An example is presented here which has been prepared by the Euthanasia Educational Council. While the Will may be disregarded if the person is in coma or heavily drugged, it does relieve the family, physician, and others of the total responsibility in making the decision to stop medical treatment.

*To My Family, My Physician, My Lawyer
And All Others Whom It May Concern*

Death is as much a reality as birth, growth, maturity and old age—it is the one certainty of life. If the time comes when I can no longer take part in decisions for my own future, let this statement stand as an expression of my wishes and directions, while I am still of sound mind.

If at such a time the situation should arise in which there is no reasonable expectation of my recovery from extreme physical or mental disability, I direct that I be allowed to die and not be kept alive by medications, artificial means or "heroic measures." I do, however, ask that medication be mercifully administered to me to alleviate suffering even though this may shorten my remaining life.

This statement is made after careful consideration and is in accordance with my strong convictions and beliefs. I want the wishes and directions here expressed carried out to the extent permitted by law. Insofar as they are not legally enforceable, I hope that those to whom this Will is addressed will regard themselves as morally bound by these provisions.

(Optional specific provisions to be made in this space)
DURABLE POWER OF ATTORNEY (optional)
I hereby designate _____
to serve as my attorney-in-fact for the purpose of making medical treatment decisions. This power of attorney shall remain effective in the event that I become incompetent or otherwise unable to make such decisions for myself.

Optional Notarization:	Signed _____
"Sworn and subscribed	Date _____
to before me	
this _____ day	Witness _____
of _____, 19 _____	Witness _____
_____	
Notary Public	
(seal)	

Copies of this request have been given to: _____
For a copy of this will, write to:
Concern for Dying, 250 W. 57th St., NY, NY 10107

CHAPTER ELEVEN

YOUR COPING STYLE

It is impossible to live without experiencing grief. Life and grief go hand-in-hand. They are entwined in the intricate web of human existence. We are involved constantly in the flow of change, and change is often connected with loss. Loss requires readjustment to a new set of beliefs, values, circumstances or concept of self. The process of grieving is the way that we release the old ways of thinking and being, and make room for the new ones. It is the way we heal after a loss.

Daily we are confronted with new ideas, products, and different ways of doing things. While integrating these changes, we experience loss as we let go of the familiar. We grieve in a small way for what we know, or for what we had, or for a person who was important in our life. Ending and beginning; birth and death; starts and finishes: these are the unavoidable rhythms and cycles that make life a totally dynamic, ever-changing process.

Life's Crises

Sometimes the events that create change in our lives are low-key and subtle. Our children grow; we learn new skills on our job; our bodies age. We don't even realize that we have changed. Other events are thunderous. They come roaring at us with such a rumble and boom that we don't know what hit us for a while. Life crises like separations, divorces, illness and death are such events, especially if they are unexpected.

Many of the events in life that create major emotional problems are normal transitions from one period to another. But they affect us strongly because of the changes they produce. We call them *crises* because they require a long period of introspection and reevaluation of self identity, values, and beliefs. Adolescence, getting married, starting a new job, changing careers, mid-life issues including menopause and climacteric (for men), and retirement are all periods of major trauma and change. These transitions often are characterized by long periods of discontent, distress and discomfort.

During these times, we search for answers to internal questions about the meaning of life, relationships, work, social pressures, and so on. Crisis is often a turning point in life when we formulate new answers and priorities. And as our lives take new direction, it is inevitable that something or someone from the past is left behind. The changes that are part of a normal life cycle always include loss. Even positive changes such as getting married or starting a new job include loss of past status of being single or unemployed.

In addition, life holds other crises in the form of death, divorce, separation, accidents, rape, abandonment, fires, and other situations that we view as tragic disruptions in the flow of life. In some cases, we are forewarned of the event. With a long terminal illness, we have time to anticipate what our lives will be like without the sick person. We can begin to grieve before the death occurs. A loved one's death is a major life change, and prior knowledge can give you precious time to more slowly and thoroughly adjust to the inescapable loss.

However, when the crisis is unexpected, such as sudden death or accident, or an unanticipated conflict, the trauma may be so great that you will undergo an extended period of instability and confusion. Your former life will be gone forever; you can never go back. Your experience will change you, for better or worse, and you will never be exactly the same as you were. How well you acknowledge and manage the changes and losses will decide how comfortably you will proceed into the future.

Most Americans believe that life is generally stable. When we talk about change, we're thinking of the small changes that affect everyday life indirectly. A new product advertised on television, a Supreme Court decision, a foreign war, or who leads the American League this week, are typical topics of conversation. We're comfortable discussing changes in politics, sports, or entertainment. But when tragedy strikes a friend or acquaintance, the news is passed on in hushed tones, perhaps couched in sympathy, and with relief that it isn't you. Often we don't know what to say to the people who are affected. It's hard to deal with personal changes in ourselves or friends.

Big changes and small changes occur all the time. Life is full of surprises; some are considered good, others bad. Because we've had painful experiences with change, or know of crisis events of others, most people see change as threatening.

When a crisis event happens in life, many people try to deny it and to resist. They see the change as an enemy to their stability. The uncertainty of *life after change* often creates resistance and anxiety. Yet crises and other major life events that force you to change can also lead to growth-producing, positive development.

It is natural for the human organism to try to avoid

pain and to look for balance. We act as if we have the option of never experiencing change and loss and grief. But we do *not* have that choice. The issue is how well we respond to changes. Even though we think that we prefer total stability, life would be pretty boring without differences and changes. Every one of us will live through the normal life transitions, and we will also experience our share of other crises.

Adjustment to Change

There are at least four possible responses to change. Let's look at them in detail.

Conservation

The first is *conservation*. This is an attempt to conserve, protect the status quo, to deny and shut out the anguish of the present pain by trying—at least mentally—to remain in the present or to return to the past. The past is idealized as the remembered state of perfect balance and harmony, a safe refuge.

This is the rigid position of the stoic who only endures the present by denying what precipitated the current crisis. The person who uses conservation as a coping stance is likely to look for others to blame as a way to understand the event. This person is unlikely to take the opportunity to alter existing behavior patterns, beliefs, or values. Passive people often use conservation as their coping style.

Polly took care of her elderly mother until she died at age eighty-nine. They lived in the same house where Polly grew up, and after her mother's death, Polly continued to live there. She kept her mother's furniture, dishes and pictures and continued most of the activities and associations that her mother enjoyed.

Polly responded to her mother's death with conservation. She never stopped to think whether she wanted to continue her life in the same way. Rather than face her own needs or desires, or her feelings about her mother, she continued in the same life, as though nothing had changed.

Revolution

The *revolution* response is to suddenly reject former values and beliefs. Security from the past seems contrived and insincere. The revolt may be against familiar people, ideas, places, society, or objects. It is another way of denying the present pain and anguish, but is a more active reaction than conservation. Conservation pulls inward rigidly, tightly, seeking safety and security. Like a clam he shuts himself inside an emotional shell. Revolution thrusts outwardly, often angrily and aggressively, rejecting the past, denying the present and damning the future.

The person who reacts to the crisis in a revolutionary way is likely to throw himself into a job or work for a cause with limitless energy and zeal, often repressing thoughts and feelings that are connected to the internal process of grieving.

He rebels and fights against everything that formerly provided stability in life, and becomes dangerously detached from all of the familiar anchors. This can eventually result in an extreme anxiety and internal stress shown in a search for new anchors, new values and new meaning in life, with no ongoing sense of self. He is adrift, alone and afraid.

Kent's wife died after a brief illness, leaving him alone at age fifty-one for the first time in his life. Her death made him aware of his mortality and aging, and he was determined not to spend his remaining years alone. He began going out quite often, to parties and nightclubs. He learned to dance and dated women much younger than himself. He stayed so busy with his new social life that he didn't develop any true, deep relationships or consider how he really wanted to spend his time. His behavior is a revolution from his former life-style, but he had not yet faced the important question of who he is.

Escape

The third possible response to change is *escape* . It is a way of evading the present anguish and pain by turning to dependent chemical or behavioral alternatives. Increased use of alcohol, drugs, sleep, food, or other addictive patterns are some ways. People who want to escape may join a cult, bask in one physical illness after another, get caught up in a social whirl, or find some other mindless way to avoid facing and accepting the uncertainty of the present and the pain of the past. The escape coping style is often used by a person who is passive-aggressive in daily interactions. He or she is fearful, insecure, manipulative, resentful, revengeful, indirect and often gives double messages. A person using this coping style tries to gain what is wanted without taking responsibility for her behavior.

This person wants to turn the self-responsibility over to anyone who will assume the position of telling her when, where, and how to live life. The escaper lives as a dependent, scared child, looking for parents to take control of her life for her. They are martyrs and the victims in society. They want to be rescued, yet when someone suggests a solution, they resent it. This approach to life is perhaps the most difficult to break. In order to alter the pattern of escape, it is necessary to stop *reacting* to events in life by using escape mechanisms and to begin to *act* in new, positive ways that are in your own best interest. Developing self-control and self-discipline is the important key for a person who wants to stop escaping and deal with reality.

Jacqueline's husband died unexpectedly, leaving the

family financial picture unresolved. Jacqueline didn't know anything about the family's finances or her husband's business, and she trusted his attorney and accountant to sort out his estate. When she received only a small amount of money, she believed the two associates had deliberately cheated her. But, still feeling helpless to take matters into her own hands, she let the matter drop. Now, years later, she complains about "what they did to me," but when she is asked why she didn't fight, she just shrugs, "What could I do?" Jacqueline has escaped responsibility for her problems and allowed others to set the rules in her life.

In order to break the patterns of dependence, begin by developing a reflective consciousness. Do not simply *react* to the crisis events in life in an instinctive, non-thinking, irrational way. Use such opportunities to reflect, think, and analyze your feelings. Decide on a positive way to resolve the problem.

Learn to Be a Survivor

Crisis events in life test our survival instincts and call upon learned coping styles of conservation, revolution or escape. Emotional reactions in human beings are connected to our most basic needs to survive and to the primitive fight-or-flight instincts in our animal nature. But what separates us from other animals is our ability to think, to analyze, to apply knowledge and intelligence to our decisions. Thinking allows us to have choices. Lower animals are at the mercy of their instincts. Human beings sometimes act the same way, as if they were solely at the mercy of the events of their lives.

In severe emotional shock, the first response is instinctive, at the emotional level. We want to deny or run away. In time, however, during the process of grieving, the emotional grip eases and our rational minds take over so that we can come to terms with our pain and begin to take control of our lives once again.

At this point we begin to think and act rationally, intelligently, as opposed to reacting blindly, irrationally and emotionally to the circumstances of our lives. We begin to break free of the destructive coping patterns.

Another Response

The fourth way to respond to crisis in life is considerably different from the first three. It is a more flexible, roll-with-the-punches way to deal with life's challenges. This position requires an openness to change and loss, views them as opportunities to gain more depth as a person, to discover more about one's self. It requires a commitment to believing that life is a process; that uncertainty is expected, that change and flux are the norm. It requires a confidence in the undiscovered parts of oneself, and a belief that one has the necessary resources to endure any life crisis.

This openness to change requires the knowledge or belief that no matter how painful the circumstances, you can feel despair and anguish and survive. This person knows that she will not perish in fear and hopelessness. She sees herself as a cork floating in a stream, sometimes basking in sunny tranquility and calm, other times caught up in its rapids, and now and then, suddenly plunged over a waterfall. But in the end, still the same cork, perhaps a little battered and bruised for the travels in life. Yet the basic essence is unchanged, enduring. And still floating, not drowned.

Transcendence

This is the position of *transcendence*. It means that you can go beyond grief and loss to reorganize your life in a new and meaningful way. The transcendent position requires a commitment to a here-and-now view of the

world. It is living in the present with honesty, openness
and flexibility to change. We cannot change the past and
we don't know the future. All we really have is right
now.

Being transcendent means trusting yourself to survive
any situation from small embarrassments to major crises. It means allowing yourself to make mistakes; to fail;
to not be perfect; to explore your feelings; to search for
your needs and desires; to ask for what you want from
others; to stand up for yourself when necessary; to love
unconditionally; to give and take; and to learn from your
mistakes. Begin to recognize your human rights, take
responsibility for yourself and act assertively in your
own best interests.

The transcendent position requires a total, complete
involvement in life as opposed to the fear, denial,
rebellion and withdrawal of the other three positions.

Compared to the other three patterns of coping and
response, transcendence strengthens and comforts you.
It is a more fully human way of being than denying,
resisting, escaping and refusing to think and feel. It is an
attitude that no matter what happens, the essence of
yourself will survive because *you* are important.

Learning to Transcend

We all use elements of these four positions to varying
degrees to cope with difficulties in our lives, but one of
the responses will be your predominant one. If your
style of coping with change in the past has not always
been best for you, you can grow to experience new
dimensions of yourself that you may never have
dreamed were part of you. You will discover untapped
reservoirs of strength and other resources.

How do you learn transcendence? By following the
suggestions throughout this book. And always by reminding yourself that no matter what or who is gone,
you must heal and survive and go on to the future.

To begin learning transcendence, Polly might take a trip or sell the family home and look for a new place to live. Kent could look for a good friend with whom to discuss his feelings about aging and start to set some goals for the next few years. Jacqueline could take legal action against the people whom she thinks cheated her. Or she could forget that chapter in her life and set about finding a way to support herself and focus on events in the present rather than the past.

All three could at least consider these options and take action on one of them when they feel ready.

Avoid Stressful Overload

Every change poses a threat to stability. Death and separation are major disruptive changes. It is more difficult when several changes come at once. Moving to a new town is an example of a complete disruption. Finding a new home, getting a job, enrolling the children in a new school, looking for doctors, dentist, accountants, and so on can be exhausting and frustrating. When such a move closely follows a death or divorce, too much of your former stability is disrupted and it is necessary to regain balance as soon as possible.

Try to monitor and regulate the number and degree of disruptions in your life at any one time. If you are headed for a stress overload, try to delay major changes for a while. Otherwise, you may be setting yourself up for sickness. It takes patience, practice and time to change.

Be kind to yourself. As you learn to be more aware of your value, more self-confident, more willing to listen and share, others will respond to you with respect, cooperation and appreciation for your openness and honesty.

RELATIVE POSITIONS OF LOSS TO SELF

Figure #1

CHAPTER TWELVE

HANDLING LOSS

Death and separation are two of the major losses that an individual may experience. The chart on page 156 explains the Relative Positions of Loss to ourselves, our fundamental identity.

The closer the relationship to the self, the more disruptive the loss.

The most profound loss is the death of oneself, or a radical change in your body, such as losing your eyesight or a limb, or a deteriorating physical illness like cancer, multiple sclerosis or others which affect physical appearance or stamina.

The second most severe type of loss is the separation from significant people in our lives by death, divorce, and abandonment. Physical attacks such as mugging or rape can be emotionally devastating, depending on the individual and on the circumstances of the event. A physical accident that requires a long recovery is also a severe loss to the *self*.

The third level of loss requiring adjustment to new ways includes the normal developmental changes of life. Some examples are adolescence, starting and/or ending school, moving, marriage, aging-related changes in your body like losing hair, reduced energy, or becoming a grandparent.

The fourth area is loss of important objects, money, hopes, aspirations, or expectations, as well as changes in the social environment such as a Supreme Court decision that may affect your life, or giving up a pet project.

With every loss we grieve. The grief is usually in appropriate proportion to the severity of the loss. When the grief is out of proportion, you may find that the release of emotions is for a former unexpressed grief or for an accumulation of losses that have not been handled and put to rest.

Grieving is the normal response to the pain and anguish of loss. It is the process of healing after a disruptive loss occurs in life. It is uncomfortable, painful, a state of dis-ease; if it is not experienced, if it is repressed or denied and internalized, it can lead to serious emotional and/or physical disease. Knowing what to expect in the process of grieving for yourself and others helps you get through the process.

We each have a unique way to grieve. There are subtle differences in our reactions, in the timing, and in the ways we approach and move through the stages of grieving.

It is impossible to be a passive observer of your own pain. It *will* hurt, and you will have to feel the pain to get past it. To learn your unique way of experiencing loss, pay attention to the way you handle smaller losses in your life. The next time you feel disappointed or irritated, watch your emotional and physical responses.

Pay attention to your thoughts and to the timing. This information will be invaluable to you when you have to adjust to a major crisis. Observe how you respond to change. Do you try to deny the loss or blame someone? Do you place obstacles in the path to healing? You may want to alter your process the next time you have to handle a loss. *Get to know yourself.*

The extent of the trauma that a loss will produce is

usually related to four important factors. *First*, to the degree of the emotional bond that you have with the lost person, place, or thing; *second*, to the type of loss; *third*, to your personality and to the way you have handled pervious losses in your life; and *fourth*, to the timing and prior knowledge of the loss. Let's look briefly at each of these factors in greater detail.

Degree of Emotional Bond

Obviously the greatest loss that we can have is our own death. The most intense and often most confused emotional relationship of our life is with ourself. The emotional relationship that we have with another person, place, or object is connected to the amount of dependency between us. Dependency is based on our basic survival needs, including the physical, emotional, mental, and spiritual aspects of our lives.

Every significant loss is like the loss of a part of ourselves in death. A great part of the fear in all losses stems, at least subconsciously, from the threat to our own survival. If we depend on a special person to take care of some of our needs, then the actual or threatened loss of that person causes a great disruption in our life, a fear that we can't go on.

If our self-image or identity is based on another person's opinion of us, loss of him may be overwhelming. This is especially true if you have been only a reflection of what he saw or wanted to see in you and haven't had a firm sense of who you really are on your own. If you have been emotionally, financially, socially, and/or physically dependent on another, the loss of that person will be very hard to handle for a while. Before you can recover, you must learn to meet your own needs.

Consider the death of a parent. A five-year-old child is dependent in every way on his mother. If she dies, he may not understand why his mother is no longer there to bathe him, to help him dress, to prepare his meals, to read to him at night, to kiss his tears away. Such a loss is total for the child. It threatens his sense of survival in a real way—others will have to take his mother's place in order for him to go on living.

Now think of the death of a parent for a forty-five-year-old woman. When her mother dies, there may be great feelings of sadness and a sense of loss, but she is likely to have left her mother's home years earlier and probably has a family of her own. She has her own circle of friends and her own means of financial support. Her mother no longer meets her primary needs. Therefore, the impact of her mother's death will be very different for her than for a five-year-old child, especially if all the conflicts between the two have been ironed out.

The case is similar in the death of a spouse. If a woman has been out in the world working, earning money, and has her own friends, she is likely to adjust more easily when her life is disrupted by the death of her husband. She has been less dependent on her husband to meet *all* of her needs. On the other hand, a woman who has always stayed at home and whose friends have been related to her husband's work or interests may find that during early widowhood she will have a greater adjustment to make. She will not have a stable support system to lean on, and she will have to learn to develop unfamiliar survival skills such as finding and holding a job, managing financial matters, etc. She is less likely to have a strong sense of herself to build on. She will need to develop many new skills rather quickly and under more stressful circumstances.

Type of Loss

The type of loss also determines your response. Losing a special person in your life has one effect while losing an important place such as a neighborhood, city, school, or place of employment affects us differently. Other types of losses may have to do with material objects such as a car, a home, furniture, recreational equipment, photographs, jewelry, or objects that have sentimental value. Changes in physical appearance can be considered a special type of loss. Aging-related changes, accidents, or surgical procedures which leave scars are losses which affect a person's self-image.

Another type of loss is the loss of a role. Roles are the most common ways that we define ourselves in our culture. Marital status, the type of job you have, the level of your education, are all social roles.

You may feel lost or confused because the role of wife is no longer available to supply the sense of identification.

The effect of role loss may be influenced by whether or not the loss is replaceable. If your wife dies, her role as wife can be filled by another woman; but the woman who was your wife is not replaceable. Some comfort and love come with the new relationship, but there may always be feelings of missing the dead person. The stronger the emotional connections, the harder the loss is to replace, even partially.

The same is true if you move to a new house. The house and neighborhood have been replaced, but not with the same room location, memories, and familiar problems as the old house. Your new house may have all the conveniences you need, but you miss the old house because of what it means to you.

If your house is burglarized and your television is stolen, it is easily replaced. Yet some objects with sentimental value are irreplaceable. Sentimental attachments are emotional attachments reminding us of special people, places or events from our past. This kind of loss is often much more upsetting than a large financial loss. It's the loss of something close to your emotional self.

Personality and Previous Losses

The third factor in how you handle loss is concerned with your personality and the way that you have managed previous losses in your life. We discussed some of these different ways of adjusting to change earlier. Let us emphasize here that almost everybody has some resistance to the pain associated with losses in their lives. We all wish that the discomfort and hurt would just go away and that life would get *back to normal*. But this won't happen. We cannot go backward. New norms will slowly emerge. Resistance only delays and drags out the inevitable.

When the loss is severe enough, resisting your healing process can lead to serious consequences. Physically, more energy is needed to fight and to deny emotional feelings than to release them. Let yourself cry, or yell, or scream to get rid of the stored-up feelings. Your feelings will try to surface over and over in the form of sadness or anger. Experience them. *Feel them.* Remember, current losses are magnified by the pain of former losses.

For example, depression is one of the serious problems of aging. Depression results from anger turned inward and from feelings of helplessness. Yet not all older people get depressed. Those who are chronically depressed have an accumulation of unresolved losses.

During life we experience many losses. If each one is handled as it presents itself, we can grow in the knowledge that a new loss won't devastate us. We can and will survive, hopefully, in a stronger and more integrated way. The person who ages successfully is one who bounces back after a loss and is able to continue living an effective and happy life.

The same is true for everyone; age, in fact, has little to do with effectively handling the losses in our lives. An infant who is suddenly weaned from the breast or his cherished thumb experiences a profound loss. The infant grieves, perhaps in a way that will become a lifelong pattern.

Birth, in fact, is the first great loss in our lives. It is a loss of a safe environment where the temperature is perfectly controlled, food is supplied, and other needs are met effortlessly. Then suddenly we are abruptly discharged and rejected from the womb. Birth is extremely traumatic. No wonder some babies are born crying.

Experts think that the way we cope and adjust to painful events is established at the time of birth at an unconscious level. And one of the challenges of our lives is to learn new and more effective ways to handle painful incidents—live through them more consciously.

Remember, we are all unique. Observe the way you handle changes, disappointments, and small losses in your life. If your process is negative and unpleasant, begin to work to change yourself. We all have the capacity to change. Learn to transcend. The first step is to be aware, reflect, and decide how you want to be. Think positively. Be a survivor. Set goals. Then do it. If you feel overwhelmed, get professional help.

Timing and Prior Knowledge

Knowing about a death or loss before it happens is an advantage. It gives you a chance to prepare for the change and loss, and to do some of the work of grieving before the actual event occurs. In the death of a loved one, anticipating what your life will be like without her is like rehearsing for the changes that you are likely to experience. You can anticipate the absence while still giving important time and attention to your loved one's last days.

It is the same with separation. The more time you have before the separation, the better. In all relationships where bonds of love are present, there is an element of loss when it ends.

You may recognize fear or feel threatened when a loved person is absent. This can happen when your spouse is away on a business trip, or when your children are out at night, or when someone you love does not get home at an appointed time. Often a little twinge of concern arises, and you may even think about what life would be like without this person in it.

This is a small grieving process. If you are extremely dependent on this person for your physical or emotional survival, your feelings of threat and fear may be profound. You may experience loneliness and separation anxiety.

Knowing about a death ahead of time has benefits, but this is not to deny the other side of the coin, which is the anguish and pain of watching someone you love slowly deteriorate before death.

The difficulty of *not* knowing or expecting the death is that there is no opportunity to prepare yourself for the loss of the person and the relationship. Therefore, all of the grief work must take place after the death, and recovery usually takes longer.

Knowledge that a loved one has a terminal disease allows you both the opportunity to complete the business in the relationship and to say goodbye. Emotional preparation can reduce the long-term impact of grief work after the death.

This does not necessarily lessen the initial trauma of the loss when it happens. Even though the death is expected, it is an emotional shock when it happens.

Choosing Life

Kings and slaves alike—and all the rest of us—experience life as a dynamic process. It is filled with imes of peace, joy, tranquility, disappointment, anger, hurt, fear, love, and much more. It is ever-changing, always in flux. Pleasure and pain are the extremes. And at some time in our lives, we experience both. Many people live most of their lives somewhere safely between the extremes, resisting change, risking little.

We each experience life with a different cast of characters, and a plot and script that varies a little from other people's. If we could step outside of the drama of our own life and view it as if we were sitting in the audience watching a play unfold before us, we probably would either be bored, feel impatient at the absurdity of the interactions of the actors, laugh or cry.

Sometimes we are moved to tears of sympathy for a sad event. In drama, human crisis is often the beginning of the play. We watch to see how the solution to tragedy will be resolved. We hope it will have a happy ending.

Often if we are detached from personal involvement in the process of our own lives, we experience life—the drama of events—only intellectually. Without feelings, we remain detached and uninvolved. We watch our own lives as if it were a play. We become spectators instead of actors in—or authors of—our own lives.

If you are detached from life, are you really alive? To be alive means to be in the state of action of life. To be involved is to be alive.

To be alive we must live wholly and experience the physical, emotional, and the spiritual dimensions of life. Imagine yourself back in the picture. You are the star, not the detached objective viewer. Your intellect does not work alone, but in conjunction with the *whole* of yourself—your physical sensations and your emotions. Life is full with feelings of joy and pain, with ongoing, unresolved questions, with activity and change and hope.

In the drama of everyone's life, tragedy strikes. It is absolutely unavoidable. The difference is how we deal

with the events and resulting pain that is associated
with the tragedy. Trouble or stress may take many
shapes and forms. It may be a separation from a loved
one through death or divorce, or just a short trip. It may
be seeing a child die. It may be losing an object that has
a special meaning in your life. It may be coming to terms
with your own aging process, or moving to another
town or making a hard decision about your career. It
may be the death by suicide of your spouse, or having a
disease or an accident that suddenly leaves you partially
paralyzed.

We all have such events to cope with in our lives. Vary
the script a little, change the names and places and
details. We all get something to resolve. In fact, we get
several somethings. In life's course, each of us has many
tragedies, crises, and trial events that are difficult and
painful.

The most significant difference among us is in the way
we react and respond to these events. The process of
readjustment is called the *grieving process*. A process is a
progressive course, a series of measures or changes that
get you from one place (psychologically) to another. It is
the opportunity to be *progressive*. Tragically, some people choose to meet the painful events in their lives
regressively, by denying, not changing, not facing the
loss.

Because grieving is a process, you will naturally move
forward and progress if you just relax and go with it. On
the other hand, if you resist and fight the work of grief,
you will eventually break down physically, mentally or,
in time, both ways.

Grief is like the Odyssey of Ulysses, full of the
unknown, through uncharted territory and internal
battles, and accompanied by fears of losing control and
of going crazy.

All human beings have to experience difficult events
in life. No one escapes living without pain in the area of

love and relationships. We all lose a loved one through death eventually. Grandparents and parents generally die before we do. Some people lose a spouse, a child, or a sibling. Loss hurts, more than anything else you'll experience.

This severing by death is so final, so irreversible, you long for the one you loved. You can't help dwelling in the past and idealizing the former relationship for a period of time after the death. However, you must accept the challenge of living life in the new way, and form new and different relationships in the here and now. Your own life cycle goes on. You cannot stop. You must keep living, moving, till your cycle is completed.

My hope for you reading this book is to let you know you do have a choice in your pain. To let you know that few people die of grief, except those who *make that choice*. Dying of a "broken heart" to follow a loved one of many years to the grave is a choice.

There is a wonderful story about being an egg or a potato. The woman who told it to me said that she thinks about this story whenever trouble comes. Many years ago when she and her husband lived in India, their six-month-old baby became ill and died. An old Indian gentleman heard of their grief and came to comfort them. He said, "A tragedy like this is similar to being plunged into boiling water. If you are an egg, your affliction will make you hard-boiled and unresponsive. If you are a potato, you will emerge soft and pliable, resilient and adaptable. Which do you want to be?" My friend says, "It may sound funny to God, but there have been many times when I have prayed, 'Oh, Lord, let me be a potato.'"

An egg or a potato? Hard and cold or warm, alive and adaptable? Many people die a slow and painful death because they choose not to grieve. They remain locked in a shell of unresponsiveness, refusing to feel, and resisting the pain and tests of life.

But remember: if you decide to resist for now, you can always choose tomorrow to feel and experience your grief; to go forward to a newer, stronger you, to a new beginning. You have to clean out the old to make way for the new. The sooner you let go of the pain and the past, the sooner you can start on your new path.

APPENDIX A

Here are suggestions for the friends and relatives of the grieving survivor.

1. *Get in touch.* Telephone. Speak either to the mourner or to someone close and ask when you can visit and how you might help. Even if much time has passed, it's never too late to express your concern.

2. *Say little on an early visit.* In the initial period (before burial), your brief embrace, your press of the hand, your few words of affection and feeling may be all that is needed.

3. *Avoid cliches and easy answers.* "He had a good life," "He is out of pain," and "Aren't you lucky that . . ." are not likely to help. A simple "I'm sorry" is better. Likewise, spiritual sayings can even provoke anger unless the mourner shares the faith that is implied. In general, *do not attempt to minimize the loss.*

4. *Be yourself.* Show your own natural concern and sorrow in your own way and in your own words.

5. *Keep in touch.* Be available. Be there. If you are a close friend or relative, your presence might be needed from the beginning. Later, when close family may be less available, anyone's visit and phone call can be very helpful.

6. *Attend to practical matters.* Discover if you might be needed to answer the phone, usher in callers, prepare meals, clean the house, care for the children, etc. This kind of help lifts burdens and creates

a bond. It might be needed well beyond the initial period, especially for the widowed.

7. *Encourage others to visit or help.* Usually one visit will overcome a friend's discomfort and allow him or her to contribute further support. You might even be able to *schedule* some visitors, so that everyone does not come at once in the beginning or fails to come at all later on.

8. *Accept silence.* If the mourner doesn't feel like talking, don't force conversation. Silence is better than aimless chatter. The mourner should be allowed to lead.

9. *Be a good listener.* When suffering spills over in words, you can do the one thing the bereaved needs above all else at that time—*you can listen.* Is he emotional? Accept that. Does he cry? Accept that too. Is he angry at God? God will manage without your defending him. Accept whatever feelings are expressed. Do not rebuke. Do not change the subject. Be as understanding as you can be.

10. *Do not attempt to tell the bereaved how he feels.* You can ask (without probing), but you cannot *know*, except as he tells you. Everyone, bereaved or not, resents an attempt to describe his feelings. To say, for example, "You must feel relieved now that he is out of pain," is presumptuous. Even to say, "I know just how you feel," is questionable. *Learn* from the mourner; do not *instruct* him.

11. *Do not probe for details about the death.* If the survivor offers information, listen with understanding.

12. *Comfort children in the family.* Do not assume that a seemingly calm child is not sorrowing. If you can, be a friend to whom feelings can be confided and with whom tears can be shed. In most cases,

incidentally, children should be left in the home and not shielded from the grieving of others.

13. *Avoid talking to others about trivia in the presence of the recently bereaved.* Prolonged discussion of sports, weather, or the stock market, for example, is resented, even if done purposely to distract the mourner.

14. *Allow the "working through" of grief.* Do not whisk away clothing or hide pictures. Do not criticize seemingly morbid behavior. Young people may repeatedly visit the site of the fatal accident. A widow may sleep with her husband's pajamas as a pillow. A young child may wear his dead sibling's clothing.

15. *Write a letter.* A sympathy card is a poor substitute for your own expression. If you take time to write of your love for and memories of the one who died, your letter might be read many times and cherished, possibly into the next generation.

16. *Encourage the postponement of major decisions until after the period of intense grief.* Whatever *can* wait *should* wait.

17. *In time, gently draw the mourner into quiet, outside activity.* He may not have the initiative to go out on his own.

18. *When the mourner returns to social activity, treat him as a normal person.* Avoid pity—it destroys self-respect. Simple understanding is enough. Acknowledge the loss, the change in his life, but don't dwell on it.

19. *Be aware of needed progress through grief.* If the mourner seems unable to resolve anger or guilt, for example, you might suggest a consultation with a clergyman or other trained counselor.

A final thought: Helping must be more than following a few rules. Especially if the bereavement is devastating and you are close to the bereaved, you may have to give more time, more care, *more of yourself* than you imagined. And you will have to perceive the *special needs* of your friend and creatively attempt to meet those needs. Such commitment and effort may even save a life. At the least, you will know the satisfaction of being truly and deeply helpful.

Amy Hillyard Jensen

APPENDIX B
Resources and Organizations

1. **American Adoption Congress**
   Box 23641 L'Enfant Station
   Washington, D.C. 20024
   Purposes are to further study, research, and teaching knowledge of adoptions and related social-psychological issues in the U.S. Publishes bimonthly newsletter; has annual conference. Regional groups.

2. **American Euthanasia Foundation**
   95 N. Birch Road., Suite 301
   Ft. Lauderdale, FL 33304
   Foundation which distributes "Mercy Wills."

3. **The Compassionate Friends**
   P.O Box 1347
   Oak Brook, IL 60521
   Non-denominational, informal self-help organization open to parents who have experienced the death of a child. Offers physical and emotional help to bereaved parents and siblings. Write for information about a local chapter. 315 chapters in U.S. Publishes quarterly newsletter. Annual convention.

4. **Concern for Dying**
   250 W. 57th St.
   New York, NY 10107
   Conducts conferences on death and dying. Education in the right to not prolong life during terminal illness. Distributes the Living Will. Publishes quar-

terly newsletter and other material. Annual convention. Regional groups.

5. **Hemlock Society**
   P.O. Box 66218
   Los Angeles, CA 90066
   Supports voluntary euthanasia for the advanced terminally ill and the seriously incurably ill. Quarterly publication plus other material.

6. **International Council for Infant Survival (Sudden Infant Death)**
   P.O. Box 3841
   Davenport, IA 52808
   4 regional groups; 26 state groups; 93 local groups. The guild offers information and consolation to members of families who have lost a child to SIDS. They also raise funds, support and encourage research, and disseminate information on sudden infant death. Publishes quarterly newsletter and other material. Annual convention in June of each year.

7. **Mothers Against Drunk Drivers (MADD)**
   5330 Primrose, Suite 146
   Fair Oaks, CA 95628
   91 regional groups; 31 state groups. Acts as the voice of the victim of drunk driving accidents. Supports Highway Patrol Programs and state and federal legislation for reform of laws on drunk driving. Counsels victims; supplies information for victims and their families on bereavement groups. Publishes newsletter and brochure.

8. **National Sudden Infant Death Foundation (SIDS)**
   Two Metro Plaza, Suite 205
   8240 Professional Place
   Landover, MD 20785

70 Local Groups; Assists bereaved parents who have lost a child to SIDS; works with families and professionals in caring for high risk infants. Supports research for public education of SIDS and related issues. Publishes semi-annual newsletter and other material. Annual convention.

9. **Parents of Murdered Children**
   1739 Bella Vista
   Cincinnati, OH 45237
   A self-help organization of parents whose children have been murdered. Offers physical and emotional support. Provides information about the criminal justice system as it pertains to survivors of a homicide victim. 35 local groups—or start your own. Publishes quarterly newsletter.

10. **Society for the Right to Die**
    250 W. 57th St.
    New York, NY 10107
    Engages in educational, judicial, and legislative activity to protect the rights of the dying patients and protect physicians, hospitals and health care providers from liability threats for complying with mandated desires of those wishing to die. Publications and annual convention.

11. **Telophase Society and The Neptune Society**
    For-profit organizations in San Diego that provide cremation and burial at sea.

12. **National Hospice Organization**
    1901 N. Fort Meyer Drive
    Arlington, VA 22209